THE HISTORICAL STORY OF ANCIENT IRELAND

Philip Lynch

MINERVA PRESS
LONDON
MIAMI RIO DE JANEIRO DELHI

THE HISTORICAL STORY OF ANCIENT IRELAND
Copyright © Philip Lynch 2000

All Rights Reserved

No part of this book may be reproduced in any form
by photocopying or by any electronic or mechanical means,
including information storage or retrieval systems,
without permission in writing from both the copyright owner
and the publisher of this book.

ISBN 0 75410 818 X

First Published 2000 by
MINERVA PRESS
315–317 Regent Street
London W1R 7YB

Printed in Great Britain for Minerva Press

THE HISTORICAL STORY OF ANCIENT IRELAND

Author's Note

As regards the geology the writer (and finder) started the study of geology in about 1928 but found in his personal research that much had to be abandoned as untenable; just mythical geology floating on mythical time. Only historical geology is tenable and, as you will see, the difficulties raised by mythical geology just melt away, leaving the scriptural account of creation and its timing completely victorious.

Philip Lynch
Feidlimidh ó Loíngsigh

I N THE BEGINNING, God created the heavens and the earth. Ours was, and remains, a separate bodied universe. For permanency, it had to be put into a rapidly revolving movement, and this caused many other kinds of motion. When this rapidly revolving movement started we call the Year of One.

The water on the face of the earth was called the deep, and it was dark until the sun heated. As all the earth began to move in orbit its first day began, and then there started the demand for a new water level for the revolving earth. This brought about the first global movement of water, towards the tropical regions, where it formed the 'great deep' mentioned in sacred scripture. This movement of water wrought the separation of the land from water, leaving a wet seed-bed for the furnishing of the earth with plants, fruit trees, grasses, et cetera. When the water had gone from the land, there continued an oozing of moisture from below that watered the growing things till the first rain started. The earth was furnished in the first six days.

The water level of the not-yet-revolving earth was, in the equatorial regions, too low by about six miles for the water level demanded by the now revolving firmament and the consequent orbiting and daily revolving of the earth. The other water of the earth had to come to fill up here to bring about the new water level. In doing this, it brought much ocean-floor mud sweepings that hardened and made divisions where the water had been moving on its way to fill up the low water in the tropical regions, and to establish the balance of weight on the earth. This movement of water on a grand scale gave stratified material, much of which hardened into rock, and this material made and maintained divisions of the water so that it was called 'seas'. The dry land was called earth.

But Ireland as we know it did not exist yet, for it is mostly a product of the pile-ups of the sweepings of the bed of the Sea of Deluge that started in the year 1656 (from the Year of One; that is 1656 AM (Anno Mundi).

Some of the first global movement of water left stratified material that hardened into rock before or after it may have been restratified – often many times. There is also an igneous erupted rock that dates from this time (1656 AM) and some of it of a later date as well. The primary stratification acted as cores to arrest the Sea of Deluge build-up, wherein material for the making of limestone was very plentiful, much having come in the general float, but of course other matter was there also: piles of floating and semi-floating debris like that which went into the making of coalfields, oil wells, gas wells, et cetera also arrested the moving flow of devastation and detritus and gave it a place to build up and to resist the current and tidal action of the gradually decreasing Sea of Deluge in its first thirteen hundred years or so.

Some layers of one-time floating material, having got covered up by other piles or layers of different or heavier material, shrank, while still retaining a water content. When the higher layers broke and subsided the water was squirted up into the hollow then formed. The historians tell us the names of the kings who were on the throne of Ireland when each lake erupted. They tell us that some erupted and flowed.

All that is laid down in one place, by water or air, is usually called a layer, but in this master layer there are minor layers, each laid down by the tide. The returning tide either made the divisions or, in doing so, brought its own variety of material and deposited it over the other deposit. As the tide takes six hours going and six hours coming it can be counted, in places exposed, the number of days, weeks, months or even years the visible part of the deposit took to get laid down.

Large causes bring about large effects in short time.

A global movement of water is a large cause, and when it goes over a world that has vegetation, animals and men who have property, roads, ports, ships, fruits, crops, turf, et cetera, the destruction is immense.

When the earth heated and the inside became molten, the polar regions became unstable, and those regions were depending on the strength of the curving crust of the 1656 AM earth to maintain their then unstable and too-high position. An adjustment in balance became necessary, so the polar regions began to come in and sink in the direction of the present shape of the earth.

As the bottom of the great deep came up in a balance of weight, the water there was pushed up and had to get back over the earth it had abandoned when it formed the seas as the first global movement of water was taking place. The air was pushed up also, and had to storm out into colder zones, releasing as it did its vast content of tropical and subtropical moisture. This is described as the floodgates of the heavens opening for forty days, for the hot air was no longer able to hold its moisture content.

The second global movement of water and the forty days' rain brought over the earth the Sea of Deluge some of which swept over the polar regions that had gone down loaded with ice fields. This water of the Sea of Deluge had some heat in it when, with speed and violence, it swept over the polar regions, where it lifted the ice fields and took a loan of them for doing some earth moving, and for bulldozing into deeper formation the flood debris.

When the earth was changing shape, the expansion of the solid crust required cracks to form, and as well as boiling up the great deep as 'fountains', these cracks made suitable exits for volcanic matter. The time this is in the fire modifies it and darkens it. As it cools, in air or in water (or both), it can crack in many ways.

This changing of the shape of the earth ensured that there would not be another universal flood, and this change took place in the year 1656 AM. The ancient Gaelic historians use this date as a pivot for dating. They record that the Gaels came to Innish Ealga (Ireland), as the De Danans told them it was called then, ten hundred and eighty years after the world was drowned. This would be 2736 AM.

The earth, because it had water on its surface, was facilitated to revolve on its axis in a day and night rotation, for the water could easily readjust the balance of weight to the changes in its own gravitational pull while it is keeping the moon from going off at a tangent. This lessens the pull on its own surface, making things lighter; and so we have high tide on the side of the earth next moon. As a person pulling a hook out of a ceiling is lighter on his heels by the amount he pulls or the strength of his pull, so the things on the opposite side of the earth become relatively lighter. This means that the water between these parts becomes relatively heavier, causing low tides. As a person pressing the surface of a cup of tea with the back of a spoon causes the surface to rise all around, the low tides' weight causes the high tides in a balance of weight, while the position and presence of the moon occasions the cause for the changing balance of weight of water on the earth. The moon does not selectively pull the water into high tide position. Water obeys earth's laws of gravity and rises and lowers in a balance of weight. The attraction of one (heavenly) body on another is not selective, it is gravitationally whole with whole on the gravity force of others. A successful pull brings about an approach. This may however require aid from another body to effect a despotic pull, as happens when sun, earth and moon are in a straight line at moon eclipse, when the moon gets so great a pull that it is helped to keep up a constant average speed, and here its own gravity pull assists. This is its orbital speed with earth as base for its speed, not its speed as it accompanies the earth, nor the speed of earth and moon with the sun as base – the sun keeping its ranks in the rapidly revolving universe where everything is in motion.

In such a universe, on the surface of an earth with such a history, Ireland as we know it began to appear as the Sea of Deluge decreased going and coming, leaving its tidal foreshore (sand and gravel) in many places on the dry-land surface. In its later stages its sand and gravel watersheds became hills and ridges which retain their very ancient name of 'uisge-cior', later just pronounced eiscir.

This same Sea of Deluge (muir an diolann) had previously piled vast layers over extensive areas of its seabed, but local currents kept these from remaining in certain places for long and so Ireland emerged from the decreasing water as an island, never joined to Great Britain by land above water. If the sea level lowered sufficiently we could walk from one to the other and to Europe on dry-land surface, but this has never been done, for Europe for years after the deluge was just called 'Isles of the Gentiles', and it took about thirteen hundred years to lower the Sea of Deluge from Ararat to near Dublin Bay (water level).

Ireland had been enriched under Sea of Deluge conditions with limestone and with much sand and gravel that was made from limestone. Large quantities of this limestone have been found to have been made from the dry-land animals that floated here – some even from the tropics or subtropics after being drowned. On its own Ireland would not have had sufficient material to give us our abundance of limestone.

They sank to the bottom of this sea that gave them time to petrify before it washed them out of their lair, broke them in pieces and rolled them around to make sand and gravel out of them before it left them high and dry. These petrified men and animals are not, of course, to be classified as natives of the Ireland that they materially enriched. The modern Irish race has preserved very well the form and features of the antediluvians, as have the animals, e.g. the Irish terrier, the Scots terrier, the Spaniel, the greyhound, the Irish wolfhound, et cetera.

Where fossils are found is now historically no guarantee that they lived there. The historical universal flood explains how heads of ostrich, giraffe, elephant, camel, snake, et cetera found their way to the gravel in the Greenhills, Co. Dublin and how tropical trees, vegetation, et cetera are in the arctic coal. Where roots of trees are found in a growing position need not warrant the deduction that they lived their life there. Floating trees keep their roots down and can settle that way in still water.

Many things have come from elsewhere to build up Ireland to give coal, gas, minerals, et cetera, brought here piled and stored by that vast historic terrible catastrophe of the universal flood of Noah, which began when he was six hundred years old. Hither also came petrified boots, turf that was cut and dried, and not frosted between the time it was cut and the time it was dried, a wooden spade and hand hoes, now stone, for planting cabbage and the like. The ancients used wood extensively as tools and also for making things and in the making of things such as soles and heels of boots and shoes, and what is thought to be the moving part of a free-wheel. Even though a man's boot and a woman's boot were found in sand and gravel at about fifty feet down we do not assert that they lived in a not yet existing Ireland, but that they were wearing them when trying to escape from drowning.

The antediluvian people, in at least some cases, were very skilful and very experienced, as their lives were long and, as is usual, the Lord provided them with geniuses, and with some who had phenomenal memories (as we find today here and there).

Great memories and long lives make an excellent setting for a flourishing and accurate historical narration, added to which the Gaels had men and institutions for preserving historical narration and severe legal penalty for introducing error. Entrance to the Bardic Order was by competition, and the best obtained the honour, revenue and privilege that legally and religiously went with it. This made for a high standard of learning and scientific accuracy as regards fact, leaving no room for replacing fact with mental theories, inventions, and conjectures for possibles to replace narrated facts, nor for denying, nor for suppressing fact on the ground of impossibility, or of blaming previous historians for inventing what they narrated. The facts they narrate have happened, the people they mention existed and had names.

Many seeds float in floods, and the Sea of Deluge was no exception, but rather it was the greatest distributor of seeds over the whole new earth's surface as its higher parts appeared. Acorns and hazelnuts got marooned in ancient Ireland, and it is narrated that a large quantity of nuts was cast up at the Boyne at Knowth (Cno is the Irish for nut). Grass seeds also came, as it is narrated that when the world explorers came to Ireland they took a handful of grass back to King Nion who had sent them. The Lord who created the world in the beginning for man's use and benefit remembered those in the ark and restored it enriched a hundredfold.

High ground gives many advantages to people and animals when there is a local flood, so the Sea of Deluge that carved out our valleys with its constant and immense currents and tides effected that Ireland, which was to have abundant rain, would at the same time have easy drainage outlets and much sandy soil to aid tillage by providing a dry or quick-drying surface. Sandhills were important in early days as were 'tells left behind by the flood' for people to live on, for Noah's race kept to high ground for long after the flood (Josephus). Gravel ridges were useful for transport, as we read that one of the five great roads to Tara followed the Esker Riada, or the gravel ridge of chariot-driving.

Ancient place names can extend from higher to lower ground as the deluge abated, as Lusticle and Lower Lusticle (Lios Ciocail, the residence of Ciocal). So did kingdoms extend farther down as we read that the beginning of Nemrod's kingdom was Babylon and Arach and Achad and Challanne in the Land of Senaar. The water there went down quickly, as it did in Ireland for a number of years, and then slowed down till it reached its present level. Nemrod was a son of Chus who was a son of Cham, son of Noah.

We read that when the people came from the East they found a plain in the Land of Senaar and dwelt there and built a city and the tower of Babel. At that time Senaar was near sea level, but now we could call it high. There was however there, as in Ireland, the law of settlement prevailing, but also builds up by lesser floods and by heavy rain, for a teem of rain in post-universal flood conditions for some years could easily leave twenty foot of debris or repeat it many times in suitable places.

It took some years to settle and harden the stratified rocks of Ireland for we have seen where the material slid while it was still unstable, and our historians, who have preserved the historical geology of Ireland, mention earthquakes and also an immense tidal wave, but now AD 1999 Ireland has so well benefited from its stratified formation that it can be considered stable and safe.

As all who came to Ireland in olden times came by boat (except Saint Patrick's leper and a celle de (a culdee) either they themselves were able to build safe and reliable boats or they came from where boats were obtainable. And, as safe boats require tools for their making and skill for their construction, we will grant that descendants of the man who was able to build the ark were quite capable men. They descended from a very long-lived man and we read of some in Ireland being long-lived (Siorna and Brendan). Long life gives experience, and with genius can accomplish much.

Whether a man was born four thousand years ago or today he has human nature and it does not change. The human race was only tenth from Adam and Eve, who were directly created by God – known to us now since He has become man as Jesus of Nazareth – when the race was again unified in Noah. It is still young.

Noah had three sons who were saved; Sem, Cham and Japheth. Most of those who invaded Ireland were descended from Japheth (Clan Seafetach). Noah had divided the world giving Sem Asia within Euphrates; Cham, Palestine and Africa; and Japheth the rest of Asia with Europe to Cadiz. Japheth's ancestors were Adam, Seth, Enos, Cainan, Malaleel, Jared, Henoch, Mathusalem, Lamech, and Noah. He had fifteen sons, Sem had twenty-seven, and Cham had thirty. One of Japheth's sons was Gomer, whose son Riphath is the ancestor of the Celts. Another of Japheth's sons was Magog whose son Bath (baah) is the father of Fenius Fear Saidh, who is the father of Niall, who had a son called Gaedeal from whom come the Gaels. From this Fenius Fear Saidh (man of wisdom *Homo sapiens*) the Gaels get the royal name of Fenians, for he was king of Scuitia (Scuit is the plural of Scot), ancient Scythia. He was eminently wise. He sent seventy-two of his people, one to each language group, and told them to report back to him in seven years. Then he took them to the Plain of Senaar where Heber's people dwelt, and there he started the famous school of universal languages at Aothenum, intending to have Gartigaran – Adam's language – as the inter-tribal means of communication, for it had not been confused at Babel as Heber refused to take part in the building of the Tower of Babel, and so afterwards the antediluvian language of humanity was called Hebrew. Heber was a son of Sale, son of Arphaxed, son of Sem.

Fenius Fear Saidh (pronounced far-sai) had two eminent scholars helping him to run the school, and these three invented three alphabets, Hebrew, Greek and Latin, and wrote them on tablets of wood. The scholars were Gar Mac Neamha (nyoa); a Hebrew, and Gadel, son of Eathoir of the race of Gomer.

Fenius gave charge of his kingdom to his son Nenual who ruled Scuitia in his absence (the Gaels were also known as the Cineadh Scuit) and he had a son, born at Aothenum where he had his university of languages. He was named Niall, and proved to be very intelligent. He was later sent by his father to found seminaries of learning in Scuitia. He got no patrimony but the benefits he got from his teaching and his learning. His name and fame spread far and reached the ear of Pharaoh Cingcris who invited him to come to teach Egypt, promising him land and revenue. He went and he so pleased Pharaoh that he gave him his daughter in marriage. She was called, as was customary, Scota, because she was the wife of a Scot. He called his son Gaedheal in honour of Professor Gadel, the Son of Eathoir.

Niall got land at Cappachiront a Plain on the Red Sea of Romar – near where the Israelites later crossed.

> On the night of the Exodus
> Through the Red Sea
> In questioning mood
> For a teacher was he
> Prince Niall met Aaron
> Who to him did tell
> The story of Israel
> And their plight then as well
> Niall said he'd help them
> And provisions supply
> He did as he said
> Though Pharaoh was nigh
> It happened that night
> That a serpent bit Gaedheal
> They rushed him to Moses
> Whose help did not fail
>
> The Leader of Israel
> Having prayed then to God
> Cured Niall's dying son
> Laying on Aaron's rod
> And said Gaedheal would go
> To a land in the west
> Where no serpents lived
> And no snakes oppressed

'Remember,' said Moses,
'The sciences to cherish'
But Niall was afraid
That by Pharaoh he'd perish
Then Moses invited
Niall's people to come
And share with the Israelites
In their God-given home
or if he preferred
He'd help him to seize
Egypt's Red Sea shipping
Till troubles would ease
With a thousand brave Israelites
Already in arms
He boarded Egypt's shipping
with the least of alarms
And saw Israel's multitude
Cross Red Sea dry-shod
In the way God had opened
And never before trod

The power of God
He saw and revered
The power of Cingcris
Need not now be feared
The Power of Egypt
Was drowned in their sight
At the dawn of the morn
of that terrible night

The Gaels got over this for the time being, for Niall and the daughter of Cingcris ruled very prudently and wisely. Gaedheal had a son called Easru who succeeded him, and Easru had a son called Sru. However,

The taking of their shipping
Egypt never could endure,
So under Sru we were banished

> By Pharaoh an Tuir (of the tower or pyramid)
> In four ships we left Egypt
> (via the Nile)
> And they took us to Crete
> where we stayed for a while.
> Sru died in Crete
> And then Heber Scot
> Took us eastwards to Scuitia
> (Though Moses said not).
> In Scuitia our fortune
> was not very kind –
> Seven years' war was the finish –
> We left Scutia behind.
> And the noble Amazonians
> (Defamed by the Greeks)
> Hospitably received us
> For fifty-two weeks.

The Amazonians, the Bactrians and the Parthians were descended from Iobhath, a son of Magog. In each of the four ships Sru had twenty-five nobles of the chiefest rank attended by their virtuous ladies.

The descendants of Nenual, son of Fenius Fear Saidh, feared that the Gaels would seek to take over the throne of Scuitia and so they harassed them until Reffleior, son of Riffil, son of Nenual who engaged Agnon the son of Tat (and son of Heber Scot) hand to hand was slain. This Reffleior had two sons, Riffil and Nenual, who after this raised a large army to drive out the royal Gaels. But the Gaels held a council and decided to go themselves as they were so outnumbered. They were led by Adnoin and Heber, two sons of (another) Tat who were grandsons of Agnamon, son of Breogamon, son of Heber Scot, son of Sru, son of Easru, son of Gaedheal. Adnoin, the father of Ealloid of Laffin and of Lughlas, died. His brother Heber had two sons: Caicer and Cing.

They set to sea westwards in three ships, three score persons in each, and every third person had a wife. They had six in command. They came west to the narrow sea that *then* flowed from the northern ocean, and in it they were caught in a storm. It violently drove them on to the *then* Island of Caronia. The water level of the Sea of Deluge was then higher than it was when present-day maps were made and when many places that have become part of the mainland were islands.

This island was then in the Pontic Sea, which has now gone down to the dimensions of the Black Sea.

The language they used was Scythian Berla Tobai, but at the request of their ancestor Fenius Fear Saidh it had been refined by Professor Gadel, who found or introduced suitable words for military men and affairs, for poetry and poets, for history and historians, for doctors and medicine, for peasants, farmers and work, and this was adopted into the family of Niall, used and kept by him and his posterity even in Egypt, and today is known (from this Gadel) as Gaelic.

The Gaels stayed a year and a quarter in Caronia. Here, Tat's son Heber and Adnoin's son Lughlas died and were buried with great grief, pomp and solemnity. Their commanders then were Ealloid, Laffin, Cing and Caicer.

The Gaels had always a sincere and great reverence for God and divine things and always held in reverence their priests, whom they called Draoi (dree). Meeting bad weather and undersea rocks, they asked God's guidance as to where they would go, and He told them, through the mouth of Caicer, that they would have no permanent home till they reached an island in the west, but that they themselves would not reach it, but their posterity would.

They received this prophecy or answer with rational and religious awe and reverence and total acceptance, and continued northwards and landed in Gotia, which was an island in the then wider Baltic Sea. Here they remained thirty years, and here Laffin had a son whom he called Heber (known to historians as Heber Gluinfhionn). Heber was his name, but as there were many Hebers, the Gaels, who preserved so well and so carefully their history, gave added names so that no error would arise in their historical narrations.

Eventually they made their way to North Africa and stayed in a place they called Gaothlaigh-Meadhonacha (géh-lee may-nagh-a). Others may have called it Gaetulia from Gaedheal? They came under Laffin and remained there under Heber (Gluinfhionn) whose descendants were Adnon Finn, Febric Glas, Neanual, Nuadhat (nooat), Alldhoid, Archaidh, and Defhatha (daha), whose son Bratha (braha) led most of his people to Spain in four transports; twenty-four men, twenty-four women and four mariners in each boat. In each boat fourteen were wedded couples and six were servants. Some did not come and their descendants are to be there till the Day of Judgement. The four leaders were Oige and Uige, two sons of Ealloid, and Mantan and Caicer.

They landed at the Bay of Corunna in north-west Spain. They found the descendants of Thubal in Spain (he was a son of Japheth). They resisted the landing of the invaders fiercely three times but in vain. A plague reduced Ealloid's son's people to ten in one day.

In the reign of Bratha and his son Breogan they had to fight fifty battles.

> Brogan the brave
> Put the Spaniards to flight –
> Victory followed him
> In every fight.
> Breogan's son Bile (billy)
> Had a son Golamh Mileadh (golu milly)
> And plain land and hilly
> Came under his sway.
> Spanish high rulers
> And Spanish high schoolers,
> Mule owners and mulers (mulateers)
> His orders obey

Breogan, to protect his people, built a city and fortified it with a wall and a trench outside the wall. From him it was called Brogan-Sciath, that is the shield of Breogan. He also built a tower now called the Old Tower. The place is called Bragansa in north-east Portugal from this Breogan.

From this king Breogan the Brigantes of Roman Britain descended through his sons who came to Ireland namely Breagha, Fuad, Muirtheimhne, Cuailgne, Cuala, Eibhle, Bladh, and Nar.

The Gaels valued, cherished and nursed friendship, especially with relatives, so Golamh asked his father's leave to go to visit their relatives in Scitia to keep alive friendship. He had proved his bravery and ability in overcoming opposition, and had made Spain peaceful, so permission was granted, and he set out with thirty well-manned and equipped ships. (It was safer in olden times when seas were not charted to travel in a fleet, for if one ship struck a rock or sprang a leak, the others could come to the rescue.)

Golamh took twelve intelligent young men with him and their task was to write down whatever they found new in astronomy, navigation, sciences and in artefacts and ways of making things. They were to work as a team and to communicate their findings to each other and to keep an exact account.

He sailed to Sicily and, by Crete, entered the Aegean Sea and the Euxine or Black Sea and up the River Tanis or Don (there is a modern town there still called Taganrog; teach an riog – the king's house).

When Golamh landed, he sent word to Reafleoir, son of Neoman, to tell his majesty who he was that had landed in Scitia. He was made very welcome and invited to court where the king himself welcomed him, trusted him, and shortly afterwards entrusted him with the command of the Scythian forces, and he gave him his daughter Seang (shang) in marriage. Here were born two of his sons, Donn and Airioch Feabhruadh (red-eyebrowed). Seang died.

His military conduct was so successful he cleared Scitia of invaders and plunderers and enlarged the territory, and was greatly loved by the people.

Reafleoir became jealous, and planned to kill him, but he got to know about it and struck first, and then left the country, taking sixty ships and their crews and landed at the Nile and sent word to Pharaoh Nectonebus (fifteenth from Pharaoh Cingcris). The king sent messengers to him, and he came into the presence of Pharaoh. He bade him welcome and gave him and his followers a territory to live in. Donn and Airioch accompanied him. When Pharaoh had satisfied himself about the trustworthiness and ability of Golamh, about his courage and military capability of opposing the attacking Ethiopians, he made him commander of his army, and his success was noised abroad throughout the nations, and Pharaoh gave him his daughter, who became known as Scota, because she was married to a Scot (a Gael or a Scythian). They had two sons in Egypt: Heber Finn and Aimhirgin. He had put the twelve young men to school in Egypt so as to be able to teach his own people when he returned.

He remembered the prophesy of Caicer and bade farewell to Pharaoh, fitted out sixty ships, set out from the Nile and landed on the island called Irena, near Thrace. Ir was born there. They went from there northwards to an island, then called Gotia, which then lay in the channel leading to the northern ocean. He stayed some time there and Colpa of the sword was born there. From there they proceeded into the narrow sea that then separated Asia from Europe on the north, and they continued in a westerly direction, having Europe on the left, till they came to Cruithentuaith or Alba. They hunted and foraged and took on provisions on the East Coast, and then proceeded to the mouth of the Rhine, whence they continued in a south-westerly direction, having France on the left. After that they landed in Biscay.

They were made very welcome and were told that the Goths and others were harassing that country and all Spain. Hearing this, Golamh landed his men, gathered the Gaelic forces and others and defeated the Goths and other tribes foreign to Spain. Having freed Spain (and Portugal) by defeating them in fifty-four battles, he took possession of the greater part of that country. Two more sons were born in Galicia: Aranan and Eiremhon (er-a-won). Heber became leader. He took the place of his father, and associated his young brother Eiremhon with him in the government. In time vast difficulties arose from a combining of the tribes against them, and their territory shrank greatly towards north and west Spain. Added to this were the effects of drought and consequent famine. Then they again thought on the prophesy of Caicer, and they knew about Ireland, so they held a council and it was considered and decided that now was the right time to go to their prophesied island and home.

They acted with prudence and fitted out a son of Breogan named Ith (eeh) with a ship and a hundred and fifty men and sent him to explore Ireland. He came ashore in the north in a storm and landed at a place called Breantracht, now called the district of Magh Iotha Mor. He enquired what was the name of the island. He was told by the inhabitants, who spoke Scythian, that it was called Innish Ealga (noble island). They told him it was ruled each year by a son of Cearmad Miorbheoil, son of the Daghda, and that the three of them took it in turns for a year, and that there was a dispute then pending between them about the crown jewels. Having got as much information as he could from them he left the ship in charge of fifty, and went to Aileach Neid – Greenan Fort in Donegal. He explained his coming to land on account of the storm and told them about his people and where they lived, and did things in so dignified, respectful and friendly a way that he made a very good impression on them through his wisdom and prudence. They accepted this noble Gael unanimously as arbiter in the matter of the treasures.

Ith's judgement was that as each one was king in his turn and as the property was their family goods, they should divide them equally. This pleased all and then he told them they had no reason to fall out with each other. The land was good and fertile, it abounded in honey and acorns, in milk, in fish, and there was an abundance of corn, the climate was not hard on the skin, and the country was large enough to make three kingdoms and fruitful enough to satisfy each king. They saw the wisdom in all this courteous, intelligent, unselfish and noble stranger said. They treated him well, were thankful to him and showed it in their friendship towards him and his hundred men and parted in friendship. It was not customary for any Gaelic leader to bring his army to the court of any monarch but to send a messenger who would inform the king who he was and why he came. (in that neighbourhood there is a place called Bogáy, (Both Iotha), the house of Ith. Perhaps the location where Ith waited.

Having courteously thanked them in the friendly Gaelic manner he departed towards where the ship was.

When he was gone a short time the brothers had a short, panicky talk among themselves. What are we doing? Did you hear how he praised the prosperity of our country? He'll go and report all he saw to his own people in Spain and they'll come to take it from us. What should we do? Bring them back is the answer and never let them go home.

Eathoir, one of the three, was sent with haste after them and had a hundred and fifty armed men with him. He caught up on the rear of Ith's men. (There is a place name some distance to the south from Drumoghill called Pringleha (priomh Gaedheal Cath) – the fight of the first Gaels. It would be on the northern side of Magh Eeh.) They had to keep to somewhat higher ground then than they would find necessary today for sea level and high tides are lower now. Ith had come to the rear and he got his men as far as Drumleen, where he made a stubborn stand, but got wounded and died on the way home. They succeeded in getting their wounded onboard before they left for home.

There is a place between Drumleen and Liffir called Rosgier (Ros Gaoith Ir); the wood of the Port of Ir. It is dry land now. Some place names still have Ith's name Magh-Iotha Mor (Maymore) (pronounced mymore), the great Plain of Ith, Maghan Iotha or Maghaire Iotha (Maherahee), the small Plain of Ith, Baile Both Mhaigh Iotha... the town of houses of Maee (Ballybofey), Cuan Mhaigh Iotha (convoy) (the inlet of Maee), Mullan Mhaigh Iotha (Mullinaveigh). Drumleen is in the Great Plain of Ith which takes in both sides of the River Foyle. Feabhal was a son of Lotan, a De Danan chief.

Ith's son Lughaidh brought his father's body back to Spain, showed it and told how he had received such wounds and how they had parted from the sons of Cearmad Miorbheoil in perfect friendship, and how they had been pursued in a hostile manner and attacked and fought, and were going to be prevented from getting back. He described the country, its strength in numbers, their weapons, their military skill, or lack of it, the type of crops, its size and its climate.

Gaelic rage was at boiling point at the treachery, abuse of friendship and unprovoked hostility, and they determined to go and punish them for that type of rascality. Added to this were famine, an amount of hostility in Spain, and the prophesy of Caicer, so they determined to go to Innish Ealga.

Golamh, who had reigned thirty-six years, died before Lughaidh returned. He was survived by his wife Scota, daughter of Pharaoh Nectonebus (fifteenth from Cingcris). Golamh was descended from Noah, Japheth, Magog, Bath, Fenius-Fear-Saidh, Niall, Gaedheal, Easru, Sru, Heber Scot, Beoghaman, Oghamhan, Tat, Agnomon, Lamhfionn, Heber Gluinfhionn, Adnon Fionn, Febric Glas, Nenuaill, Nughatt, Alldhoid, Earchada, Deaghatha, Bratha, Breogan, and Bile, who was his father.

The Gaels got ready thirty man-o'wars with thirty warriors in each, and not willing to leave behind them any of their considerable fleet nor lifeboats nor landing craft, they had with them seventy-five ships and counting large and small of all kinds they had a hundred and fifty. The fleet was well equipped, well manned and well supplied for the journey, and they were as a people coming to their home. When Red Hugh O'Donnell went to Spain for military help after the Battle of Kinsale, in AD 1602, he considered it a good omen that he had come to the place from where his ancestors had come to Ireland, and he went to see Breogan's Tower.

They set out from Spain ten hundred and eighty years after the world was drowned; that is two thousand, seven hundred and thirty-six years after the creation of earth, sun, moon and stars, and the furnishing of the earth.

The wind was favourable. When they appeared at Lough Garman (Wexford), the De Danan magician deceived them by making the land look as if it was a huge pig, so they went south and west to what was later called Invir Sceine (Bantry Bay), where they landed on 17th May. At Slieve Mis (mish), which is near Tralee, it was agreed to send an embassy to the sons of Cearmad, and Aimhirgin was chosen to be the spokesman. There they met Banba, the wife of Eathoir, who said who she was when questioned by Aimhirgin. Answering in a polite and dignified way she told them that her name was Banba, and it was from her that Innish Ealga was called Banba (poets still use this name).

They all marched on to what was later called Slieve Eibhlinne (son of Breogan) where they met the wife of Teathoir. She also had a retinue of Ladies and Draoi. When Aimhirgin requested the honour to know her name, she courteously replied that her name was Fodhla (folla), and that from her the island was called Fodhla.

They went on to Uisneach, where they were met by the wife

of Ceathoir, whose name was also asked. Ladylike, she replied that her name was Eire and from her the country was called Eire.

These three were sisters. They were daughters of Fiacha, son of Dealbhaoith, son of Oghma, and their mother was Einin, the daughter of Eaderlamh. They were married to the three sons of Cearmad, son of the Great Daghda, son of Ealatha, Dealbhaoith, Neid, Iondaoi, Alloai, Tait, Tabhairne, Eana, Bath, Iobath, Beothach, Iarbhainel Faidh, Nevy, Adnamhan, Pamp, Tat, Seara, Sru, Easru, Framant, Fathochta, Magog, Japheth, son of Noah.

They went on to Liathdrum, afterwards called Tara, and met the three brothers, sons of Cearmad and demanded the rule of the island as an eric for having attacked Ith (eeh) against all signs of friendship. They replied, 'You have broken the Law of Nations by invading without giving notice in advance.'

This was admitted by the law-abiding Gaels.

'What is to be done? We will accept Aimhirgin as judge, but not if he gives an unjust judgement. We have broken International Law. We will have to go back nine wave-lengths from the shore.'

'If you go back nine wave-lengths from the shore and can then effect a landing, we'll surrender to you the sovereignty of the island.'

They did this, and then a terrible storm suddenly arose, which Donn and Aimhirgin said was a druidical wind, and the De Danan Draoi used magical powers, and knew this wind was the result of their doings.

Aranan, Golamh's youngest son, climbed the mast to see how many were there to oppose them when landing, but the storm caused him to fall and he was killed. Donn, his brother (his mother was Seang), was in a boat that was separated from the rest when the ship was smashed and with him were drowned twenty-four soldiers, four galley-slaves, twelve women, fifty Gaels who went as volunteers and five captains, whose names were Bille, son of Brighe, Airioch Feabhruadh, Buan, Breas, and Cualgne. Ir, son of Golamh, and all hands perished in his ship. Ir's body was washed ashore and he was buried on Sceilg Mhithill. He was very brave and a great defender in battle and his descendants became known as the Red Branch Knights (the Clanna Rudhruidhe).

Great confusion reigned and the whole fleet was in danger.

Eiremhon managed to save a large number of the fleet and came to the mouth of the Boyne, but his brother was drowned landing. The town of Colpe (Cope) gets its name from him, and the mouth of the Boyne gets its name from him also; Invir Colpa.

Three days after Heber Fionn succeeded in coming ashore they were attacked by Queen Eire with a large body of men at Slieve Mis (mish). Both sides fought desperately, the De Danans lost a thousand, the Gaels three hundred, among whom was Golamh's widow, Scota. Glen Scoithin is named after her and her tomb is there. Fas also died, from whom Glen Fais is named. She was the wife of Un, son of Uige. Two Draoi, Uar and Eithir, also fell.

Queen Eire retired with her beaten troops and went to Telltown, but the Gaels stayed there entombing their dead. They celebrated with great reverence and solemnity the funeral rites of the learned Uar and the draoi Eithir who fell side by side, helping as best they could. Aimhirgin's wife Sceine was drowned, and from her, Invir Sceine is named (now Bantry Bay). Bille's wife Buan was drowned, as was Dil the wife and half-sister of Donn. The Gaels having sorted themselves out and seen to the wounded started, under Heber Fionn, to rejoin the rest, and they joined forces at Invir Colpa. When they were ready, they sent word to the sons of Cearmad to give up the kingdom or come to battle. They left the boats in such a state that there would be no return to Spain. The De Danans gave answer that they would contest their demand, and the Battle of Telltown ensued.

The De Danans began the fight and were received with great bravery. Both sides held their ground with no give on any side. Ceathoir fell by Aimhirgin, Eathoir by Eiremhon, and Teathoir by Heber Fionn. Eire was slain by Suirghe, Fodhla by Eatan, and Banba by Caicer, son of Manntan.

When the three royal De Danans were slain their army gave way under very great pressure from the Gaels, who pursued them hotly and far, and lost two of their brave generals in the pursuit – Cuailgne, son of Breogan at Sliabh Cuailgne and his brother Fuad at Sliabh Fuaid.

The Gaels, like the Hebrews, had many a hard struggle for existence and for freedom and had of necessity to maintain a military alertness, but they gave much attention to the arts and crafts, to historical narration, to learning, to religion, and to continuous genealogy. They preserved the account of their own historical origin from the first man, Adam, and the first woman, Eve, who were formed and created the same day of the first week, and lived their lives as man and wife and started to propagate the human race. The Gaels also preserved the historical geology of their country in the world that had been drowned.

It was a Gaelic custom to bury their dead with public respect and to mark their graves or build their cairns, and also to build the cairns of the defeated, and these were treated as dignified foes while the battle was in progress and as free human beings when fight was over. The rights given by Brehon Law were known and respected by victor and by vanquished. Any dishonourable conduct was lashed by the bards, so the Gaels put death before dishonour, and historian bards kept the memory of brave and noble deeds, and later bards were wont to refer to these, and so a glorious deed shone with brightness on his or her people.

After the Battle of Telltown, the Gaels took over the ruling of Ireland, and Heber Fionn and Eiremhon became its kings.

Heber built his palace at Rath-Loamhuin, and Eiremhon built his at Airigidross on the Nore (Rath-Beitheach).

This ruling arrangement only lasted a year. Heber's wife wanted to be queen of the three most fertile ridges in Erin, and as one of these lay in Eiremhon's part, she sent Heber to ask it. But he would not consent to that, so Heber returned without it and was sent again under threat that she would go back to Spain if she did not get it. So the Battle of Geisiel was fought between Heber and Eiremhon and their forces. Heber lost three of his chief officers, Suirghe, Sobhairce and Goisdean, and he was mortally wounded himself and died at his brother's palace at Airigidross.

About a year after Heber died the fierce fight of Cul Caicer was fought. Caicer was one of Heber's chief officers and was killed by Eiremhon. In the year following Caicer's death the Battle of Bile Teineadh was fought, in which Aimhirgin was slain by his brother Eiremhon. Inside three more years Manntan and Fulman – two other officers of Heber – were slain at Breaghuin in Freamhain.

Before the Battle of Bile Teineadh took place a number of important women had died; Scota, Fas, Tea (the wife of Eiremhon from whom the royal residence at Liathdrum was called Tara (Tea-Muir, the wall of Tea), for she chose it for her residence), Fial the wife of Lughaidh (a woman of strict virtue and great modesty, so confounded that her husband had seen her naked as she had a swim in a river, now called Abhann Feile, that she languished and died of shame), Liobhradh the wife of Fuad (a son of Breogan), Sceine wife of Aimhirgin, Buan wife of Bille, Dil wife of Donn, and Odhbha, who had been married to Eiremhon and who was interred on a hill on the Ardbraccan side of Navan (Cnocan Odhbhan). Feminine modesty made the Irish nation great.

The Battle of Telltown had been against a foe, but Geisiel was fratricidal, as were Cul Caicer and Bile Teineadh.

When Eiremhon was sole monarch he gave the two Munsters, North Munster and South Munster, to the four sons of his dead brother Heber: Er, Orbha, Fearon, and Feargna. He gave Connacht to Er, son of Uige and to Eadan (two generals). Ulster he gave to Heber, the son of his brother Ir. He gave the province of Leinster to a worthy person of the Fir Bolg race, whose name was Criomhtan Sciathbheal (skeevell).

Early in Eiremhon's reign a general called Gud led three hundred men to this country. He had come from Thrace and had served under Policorn. He had a beautiful daughter, but when he heard that this effeminate, wicked man was going to use force to take her as a concubine he, with the aid of the Picts who were under him and who were not in favour of doing any such thing to a decent girl, slew him and fled from Thrace. He crossed many countries and was received in a friendly way by the king in France. They lived in and around the place where they built a town which is called from them Poitiers. The king of that country, moved by the desire of debauchery, was going to use force on her also, but Gud found out in time and by a stratagem seized French shipping and came to Ireland and landed at Invir Slaine (Wexford). The girl (now a woman) died on the voyage. They were received with hospitality and with friendship by Criomhthan. They requested somewhere to stay, which was a matter for the Ard-ri (ard-ree).

A tribe of Britons who were known as Tuatha Fiodhga (fee-o-ga) were plundering part of his territory that lay around Wexford and attacking with poisoned arrows or weapons that wounded lethally. Criomhthan (criffin) asked the Picts if they knew any way of countering this and they referred him to Trosdan. He told them to dig a hole where they expected the next fight and to put into it the milk of a hundred and fifty hornless cows and get his wounded men to bathe in it and it would extract the poison. This battle was called Cath Arda Leamhnachta and the place was known as Ard Leamhnacta (height of new milk). They followed the prescription of this chemist and it proved so successful that they were able to go back to the battle and beat the Britons.

After this, the Picts under Gud and his son Cathluan were found to be making political moves aimed at territory in Leinster, so Criffin sent word to the Ard-ri. Eiremhon's show of force was sufficient to encourage them into humble submission and friendliness.

Eiremhon withdrew, but told them there was a country to the north east to which they could go. They decided to go, and he sent troops with them to help if need arose, but before they went they requested that he supply them with what they needed – wives. 'We are only men,' they said and Eiremhon did not let them down. He told them there were young widows of the Tuatha De Dananns whose husbands were killed a short time ago. They were glad and got fixed up. The leaders got three Gaelic widows: the wife of Breas (one of the three sons of Tighearnbard (tee-earn-bard)), the wife of Buas, and the wife of Buaighne. The son of Gud, Cathluan, became the first Pictish king and there were seventy of them.

> "Twas Cathluan began the royal line
> Which ended in the hero Constantine.'
> As then agreed so it has been.
> They all descended from a Gaelic queen
>   (real mac Guidh)

Twenty-four skilled men who came in the invasion cleared plains for crops and these plains are known by their names (Magh (ma) is the Gaelic for a plain), Magh Aí, Asal, Meidhe, Morbha, Meide, Cuibh, Cliu, Ceara, Reir, Slan, Leighe, Liffe, Line, Leighean, Trea, Dula, Adhair, Aire, Deisi, Deala, Fea, Feimhin, and Seara.

The sons of Breogan, when it was seen that the friendly Picts had been successful, requested Eiremhon to let them go also, and he fixed them up in Cumberland. They were known to the Romans in Britain as Brigantes (Gael-Brit).

Six of the learned Picts remained in Ireland: Trosdan, Oilean, Ulpra, Neactan, Nar, and Eneas. They were given land in Meath by Eiremhon.

There had been a difficulty between Heber Fionn and Eiremhon in deciding whose should be the poet Cir Mac Cis, and whose the musician Onaoí, but they agreed to settle it by lot and Heber got the bard.

*

The following account was received by the Gaels and preserved carefully for their people concerning what had happened in Ireland before they came to it ten hundred and eighty years after the world was drowned by the Sea of Deluge in the year 1656 AM. The Gaels being curious and careful to find out all they could about Ireland that they knew as their prophesied home, learned that a man called Ciocal son of Nel, son of Garbh, son of Uadhmhor (oo-wor) with his mother Lot Luaimneach (nimble) had lived here about two hundred years after the world was drowned, and lived on fish and fowl, and that a man called Partholon, who had killed his father and mother in his effort to get the throne of Greece (and to prevent his older brother from getting it) had also come here.

Partholon had started from Migdonia (a district in Macedonia), steered by Sicily, sailed across what is now France, with Spain on his left, and landed at Invir Sceine (Bantry Bay) on 14th May. With him came his wife Dealgnait, his three sons Slaine, Rughraide and Laighline, their wives and a thousand soldiers.

Ciocal fought them at Magh Ith but was defeated. He had come in six ships – fifty men and fifty women in each, and had landed at Invir Domhnann. His name survives in Lusticle (Lios Ciocail = Gaelic. House of Ciocail = English) in Magh Ith.

Partholon's people were here for three hundred years, having come about three hundred years after the world was drowned in 1656 AM. Their colony perished by a plague – five thousand men and four thousand women in one week; 'they died in flocks on the Plain of Flocks' (of birds) and their grave is known as Tamleacht Mhuintir Phartholoin (the plague-grave of Partholon's people). That part of the plain was later distinguished from other plains as Magh Ealta Eadair, but earlier it was called Seanmhagh Ealta for it was barren from the sand and gravel of the Sea of Deluge. This man, Partholon, died thirty years after coming, and left four sons, Er, Orbha, Fearon, and Feargna, who divided the island between them (the four sons of Heber Fionn had the same names). Their friendship, agreement and brotherly love persevered from the time they were children till old age. Partholon also had ten daughters whom he married to ten noblemen of his colony.

The brothers who came in the flight from Migdonia died; Slaine when here about thirteen years, and interred at Sliabh Slaine, Laighline a year after that. As his grave was being dug Loch Laighline sprang out. After the layers that were laid down by the Sea of Deluge settled very gradually and admitted water in between them, subsidence of the upper layer, or layers, was apt to take place and also squirting up of the trapped water, for some layers shrank more than others or had a greater water content. The water erupting, being under great weight and consequent high pressure, could and did drown those caught by it. Rughruidhe was drowned by Loch Rughruidhe, where the land sank and became a lake.

When Partholon came he only found three lakes: Loch Luimneach, Loch Ceara, and Loch Foírdreamhuin (now Tralee Bay) and nine rivers: Lee, Buas, Bearbh, Banna (Upper and Lower Bann of today were one river then), Saimer, Sligo, Modhorn, Muadh (Moy) and Liffe. In Partholon's time seven lakes burst out: Lough Measg, Loch Con, and twelve years after his coming, Loch Deichiod (Gara) began to flow. Loch Laighline sprang out of a hole two years after that, next year Loch Eachtra erupted, then Loch Rughruidhe, and in the same year Loch Luain erupted and began to flow.

With Partholon came four learned men: Lag, Lagmhadh, Iomaire, and Eithrighe, three draoi: Fios, Eolas, and Fochmair, three generals: Muca, Mearan and Munichneachan, and two merchants: Biobhal and Beabal. One man called Beoir introduced feasting and drinking, and Samalilath obliged by making cups. Breagha introduced single combat, he was a son of Seanbhoth.

The Gaels were told that this people were ruled wisely.

When Partholon's wife was unfaithful (even so short a time after the world was drowned for sin and she could see such evidence of sin's punishment) he vented his rage on her dog, Saimer, which he caught up and hurled to the ground with such violence that he killed it. The place still bears the name of the dog. When reproached by him for this crime of adultery with Todhga (tow-a), her servant, she responded with lines from a poet who had prostituted the poetic art in a way that debased her, and Partholon, having killed his father and mother, held back from killing her.

There was a baby son who did not come with his father, Partholon, in his flight from Greece and his successors, led by Neimheadh (Nevy) came from the Euxine Sea to where their relatives who had not been killed by the plague had been (the surname MacPartholon exists in Leitrim).

Nevy came to Ireland six hundred and thirty years after the Deluge. Nevy came in thirty-four boats, thirty people in each, passed by Sleibhte Riffe (Mount Riffe) on his left and came to a place called Aigen in the north, and then to Ireland. His four sons, Stairn, Iarbhanel Faidh (the Prophet), Ainnin, and Feargus Leithdhearg came with him, as did Macha his wife. She died after twelve years and before her son Ainnin. He buried her in Ard Mhacha. Armagh is named from her.

There was another Macha the wife of Cimbaoith. She was Gaelic and she ruled near Armagh at Eomhuin Mhacha (Navan Fort), the historians call her Macha Mongruadh (red-haired).

A people had come to Ireland from Africa, said to be descended from Sem son of Noah, and they were known to the Irish historians as Fomhoric (four-ik). They said their reason for leaving Africa was to get away from all association with the descendants of Cham, son of Noah, for fear they might also be implicated in the disadvantages of Noah's curse. Those in Ireland regarded them as sea-robbers. They made Torry Island their headquarters.

Nevy built two elegant palaces and employed four skilled men of the Fomhoric: Bog, Robhog, Rodin, and Ruibhne. They were sons of Madan Muinreamhar (fat necked), and so proud and satisfied was Nevy that he did not want anyone else to get them to erect as good (or better). He contrived to have them killed at Doire Lighe (Derrylea in County Armagh), and they are buried there. This did not foster friendship...

Nevy fought them and beat them in three battles: Sliabh Badhna, Ros Fraochan, and Murbolg, but in this last he lost his son Stairn, who was slain by Conuing, son of Faobhar. Another desperate engagement was fought at Cnamross in Leinster and most of his forces were cut to pieces. He lost his son Artur, and also his grandson Iobhchon (eev-hon). For Nevy, the results were Pyrrhic. He died soon after at Ard Nevy (Barrymore Island) with two thousand of his people of a plague. The Fomhoric, taking advantage of his loss at Cnamross and Barrymore, gathered their forces and took over the domination of Ireland, and compelled Nevy's people to pay a heavy tribute, which one of the Fomorian women had charge of collecting or of extorting every first of November. She demanded of every family three large measures of wheaten meal, three measures of cream, three measures of butter, two parts of their cattle and of their children.

Morc, son of Deileadh (a Fir Bolg) and Coning, son of Faobhar equipped a large and strong fleet and kept a standing army and by these the natives were compelled by force to bring the tribute to them to a plain between the Erne and the Drobhaois. This plain was called Magh Gceidne (or the plain of compulsion).

Before Nevy died he had cleared twelve plains of trees, et cetera for tillage and use. These were: Magh Ceara, Magh Neara, Magh Cuile Tola, Magh Luirg, (in Conacht), Magh Tochair, Magh Breasta (in Leinster), Leacmhagh (in Munster), Magh Lughaidh, Magh Seireadh (at Sletty), Magh Seimne (near Larne), Magh Muirtheimhne and Magh Macha.

Four lakes erupted in Nevy's time: Loch Breanuin, Loch Muinreamhair, Loch Deirbhreach, and after fourteen years Loch Ainnin began to flow.

Being oppressed harshly, Nevy's people consorted efforts to meet the Fomhoric in battle, and they gathered thirty thousand on land and thirty thousand on sea. Their generals were Beothach, son of Iarbhaniel, Fathach, son of Nevy and his brother, Feargus Leithdearg. Three outstanding warriors, Earglan, Mantan and Iarthacht, sons of Beoan, son of Stairn, son of Nevy, volunteered to lead where the foe was strongest. They attacked when Morc (Mork) was away in Africa and they killed Conuing and his family and destroyed his garrison. But Morc returned with sixty ships and a large number of soldiers and Nevy's people tried hard to prevent them from landing on Torry Island. So furious was the fight that the incoming tide drowned a large number of them when making for land. Only one boat with thirty officers of Nevy's people escaped.

Three of their generals who escaped were Simon Breac, son of Stairn, Iobhach, son of Beothach and Briotan Maol (Bald), son of Feargus Leithdearg. They made their way back to Ireland and were very oppressed with slavery, so they came to the resolution to quit Ireland, but it took seven years till they got the opportunity to go. Morc gathered together what remained of his forces and took possession of Ireland.

These three divided the old boats that Nevy had come in and departed. Simon went to Greece where he and those who went with him were made to work hard to shift clay from the valleys and carry it up the hills that the tides of the Sea of Deluge had left there and had left bare of soil. The idea was to make the hills fertile so as to grow useful food, et cetera.

Iobhach and those who followed him sailed towards northern Europe but eventually gravitated to Greece (some said that it was to Boetia (Bothany) in northern Europe that he went). Briotan Maol took his people to Alba, but these gradually spread south, and from him the country was called by the name of Britain, and part of it by the name of Wales (from Maol), but that was afterwards. Some of his people were in Alba when the Picts arrived, and he spent some time in Dobhar and Iardobhar.

The number of boats they divided before leaving, if we count all kinds, even those covered with skins of leather – curraghs, naomhogs, skiffs, et cetera, was eleven hundred and thirty. Not all went and those who remained were greatly oppressed by the Fomhoric until relief came.

Five brothers, Slaine, Rughruidhe, Gann, Geanann, and Seangann, sons of Deala, son of Loich, Triobhuaith, Othoirbh, Goisdean, Oirtheacht, Simon, Arglamh, Beoan, Stairn, Nevy, Adnamhuin, Pamp, Tat, Seara, Sru, Easru, Fraimint, Fathochta, Magog, Japheth and Noah, seeing themselves and their kindred under so great servitude in Greece, for they were oppressed like the Israelites in Egypt, (of fear that they would take over the government), privately agreed that they would leave Greece; 'Ta an domhan Mor' (the world is big). They fitted out what boats they could lay hands on. They used the leather bags that they carried the clay in and repaired curraghs, skiffs and naomhogs, et cetera all to the same number as Simon and his brothers divided before they left Ireland. They set to sea with five thousand followers, and in three days reached Spain in fair weather. They reached Ireland, with fair weather, in thirteen days. Slaine landed at Inver Slaine on a Saturday, Gann and Seangann at Iorrus Domhnain (Mayo) the following Tuesday, Geanann and Rughruidhe on that Friday at Traght Rughruidhe (the inner bay of Dundrum in County Down).

Slaine's contingent was known as Fir Bolg (men of bags). Gann and Seangann's two thousand were known as Fir Domhnoin, for they did the digging, and the spear-men who defended them and others from wild beasts, et cetera, were known as Fir Gaileon. Historians generally refer to all who came then as Fir Bolgs. Slaine was married to Fuad, Gann to Eadar, Seangann to Anust, Geanann to Cnuca, and Rughruidhe to Liobhra (leev-re). We notice that an odd name is used by a man or a woman. They had set out from Greece on a Wednesday. The historians narrate that they came to Ireland two hundred and seventeen years after Nevy landed.

Ireland was divided by them: Slaine got from Invir Colpa (Boyne) to Cumar na dTri nUisge (Waterford); he was the youngest. Gann got to near Cork, Seangann to near Limerick,

Geanann to the Drowes (south-west Donegal), and Rughruidhe got Ulster. Each got a thousand of those who came to Ireland.

Slaine was High king for a year and he was the first of them to die. He was buried in Dumha Slaine (west of the Barrow). Then Rughruidhe took the kingship for two years till he was drowned at Brugh os Boinn (Newgrange). The water was higher then. Geanann and Seangann then reigned for four years together. After them, Gann reigned five years till slain by Fiacha Cinnfionan, son of Stairn, son of Rughruidhe (Rory), son of Deala, son of Loich; and he was slain himself by Riondal, son of Geanann, son of Deala.

Riondal reigned six years and fell in battle slain by Fiodhbhghean (feev-yen) at a place called Craoibhe (there is a Creeve near Lower Bann), Feeveyen reigned four years till slain in battle by Eochaidh Mac Eirc, son of Riondal, at Muirtheimhne (Dundalk). Feeveyen was a son of Seangan, son of Deala. Eochaidh Mac Eirc, son of Riondal, reigned ten years. In his reign there was no rain nor bad weather but neither fruit nor crop failed, as there was a heavy dew. He enacted laws to keep his people in peace and security of life and of property and set sanctions to have them kept.

Tailte was the wife of king Eocaidh Mac Eirc; she was a daughter of Maghmor, a king in Spain (Spain and Portugal now). Telltown gets its name from her because Tailte was buried there. The Fir Bolg held Ireland for thirty-six years. (As regards no rain, conditions were then not as stable as now.)

Whilst Iobhach and his people were in Greece, they learned arts and crafts and skill in magic, not, of course, all of them, but four out-standing names are mentioned: Moirfhias, Arias, Erus, and Semias, and these were teachers.

The magical powers of the De Danans (who were next to come to Ireland) greatly helped the Athenians against the Syrians who had come in a large fleet against them, but when the Syrians consulted their own draoi he told them how to counter the De Danan magic and how to find out if their power was from God or not. He told them if it was from God nothing would master it. His guidance was successful, so when this happened the De Danans fled for their lives as best they could under their leader

Nuadha, who kept them as safe as he could till they reached Norway-Sweden, then called Lochlonn or Fionn-Lochlonn (fionn means fair or blond). The word finn is still in the word Finland. The Fionnlochlannaigh made them welcome, treated them with respect and religious reverence on account of their skill and ability. They got four cities and in these they started schools to instruct the youth of the country as well as their own. Moirfhias taught in a town called Failias, Arias in Finnias, Erus in Gorias, Semias in Murias. There is a Greek flavour in the end of these words.

After remaining some time with those hospitable people and having instructed many of them, they decided to go farther west. They spent seven years in Alba around Dobhar and Iar Dobhar, and then they invaded Ireland:

> They land on the shore
> Their boats they burn
> Here for evermore
> Never to return
>
> Give half the kingdom
> Or in battle contest
> King Eochaidh Mac Eirc
> We speak not in jest
>
> Enemy so daring
> This kingdom we own
> You won't burst our mearing
> While flesh's on our bone
>
> In thousands they're numbered
> The men who are slain
> The Fir Bolg encumbered
> (South) Moytura's Plain

> They died fighting bravely
> Against the invaders
> Spilling their life-blood
> Repelling these raiders.

They gave no warning beforehand but landed stealthily and had got as far as Sliabh an Iarann (Co. Leitrim) before sending to king Eochaidh their demand. The contest took place near Cong and from the mounds raised over the fallen it was called Magh Tuireadh (Theas). Eochaidh was slain and the leader of the De Danan army, Nuadha, lost his hand. It took seven years in all between healing it and fitting him with a satisfactory silver hand; hence he is known to historians as Nuadha Laimh Airgid. He reigned for thirty years, but Breas was in charge for the seven years he was getting rid of his 'blemish'. Miach was his surgeon, and Creda was his silversmith who did the work so well that when finished he was able to take over the full kingship. This, however, did not go down well with his cousin Breas, but he had to take it then and for twenty more years. When he allied himself with the Fomhoric and others, in an effort to get the throne of Ireland, and when they were here about thirty years, he lost the Battle of North Moytura fighting against his own people.

In this battle king Nuadha's head was cut off, slain by Ealadh and by Ballar na Neid. Nuadha was the son of Eachtach, Eadarlamh, Ordan, Allaí, Taít, Tabran, Eana, Baath, Iobhath, Beothach, Iarbhaniel Faidh and Nevy. The De Danans won and oppressed the vanquished. The De Danans landed in Ireland on the first Monday in May bringing with them the Lia Fail (stone of destiny) that they brought from the town of Failias, the sword of Lugh Lamhfhada from Gorias, his spear from Finias and a famous cauldron that was known as Coire an Dadhda.

There were two outstanding women of them: Beachoil and Danann. Danann was the daughter of Dealbhaoith, Elathan, Neid, Jundaoi, Allaoi, Tait, Tabhairn, Eana, Bathath, Iobhath, Beothach, Iarbhaniel Faidh, Neimheadh (Nevy) and she was the mother of Brian, Iuchar, and Iucharbha (u-har-oó-a). From her comes the De Danan name but the De comes from their exceeding great skill in art, craft and magic. They were regarded as just a bit more than the ordinary run of humans.

Nuadha was the son of Euchtach, Eadarlamh, Orda, Allaoi, Tat, Tabhairn, Eana, Bathach, Iobhath, Beothach, Iarbaniel Faidh, Nevy. He was succeeded by Breas, son of Ealatha, son of Neid, son of Jundaoi, who reigned seven years. Breas was succeeded by Lugh Lamhfhada, son of Cian, Diancheacht, Easar Breac, Neid, Jundaoi, and he reigned for forty years. He was fostered and trained by Tailte, a daughter of Maghmor, a king in Spain.

She was the widow of Eochaidh Mac Eirc and married Eochaidh Garbh, son of Duach Dall, a chief of the Tuatha De Danans.

To honour her memory Lugh (Lamhfhada) started the Tailtean Games, and they went on from a fortnight before till a fortnight after 1st August (called in Gaelic, Lughnasagh, for nasadh is a commemoration). He was slain by 'Mac' Cuill (Eathoir) at Uisneach (Coll means a hazel; he had got a present of a very famous shield that Manannan made from a dripping, ancient hazel that was associated with Balor). He is said to have introduced cavalry into Ireland.

Eochaidh Ollathar ruled seventy years. He is known as the Great Daghda and is son of Ealatha, Dealbhaoith and Neid son of Iondaoi. He died at Brugh-os-Boinn from the effects of things thrown at him by Ceithleann at the Battle of North Moytura.

The Daghda was succeeded by Dealbhaoith, son of Oghma Grian Eigis (eigis is learned), son of Ealatha, son of Dealbhaoith, son of Neid. He ruled for ten years. He was killed by Fiachaidh, son of Dealbaoith, son of Ealatha, who succeeded him for ten years till slain by Eoghan at Ard Breac. Then the three sons of Cearmad Mirbheoil (also written Milbheoil), son of the Daghda, ruled in turn each for a year and held the sovereignty thirty years till slain in the Battle of Telltown defending Ireland against the Gaels, ten hundred and eighty years after the world was drowned.

By that time the De Danans had been in Ireland a hundred and ninety-seven years and had the country in a very prosperous condition, for there was plenty of honey, fruit, milk, acorns, fish and corn as we learn from what Ith (Eeh) told them when he was instructing them to consider how blessed they were in having so favoured a country that was large enough for them all, and that friendship and fraternity could and should prevail amongst them in such a good climate. This advice was given in the year of the world 2736, and the Gaelic invasion took place the following year – 2737 or 1260 BC.

Diancheacht was a doctor. Luchtaine was an engineer. Goibhneann was a smith. Cairbre, son of Tara, son of Tairreall, was a poet. Bridhid was a poetess. They were well organised on a military footing, they beat multitudes of the Fir Bolg and thirty years after that beat the Fomhoric in Breas's conspiracy. At North Moytura, Balor used the evil eyes on them. With them he poured jets of a very evil substance out of his eyes and these jets, going straight, like rays, hit the enemy in the eyes with lethal effect. The evil substance had the colour of a cancer scab. It was hellish, and the De Danans narrated that he was able to kill with it. They thought that it was in the forehead or somewhere about the head and they referred to it in the singular and spoke of him as Balor of the evil eye. It is at its most effective distance at about five to seven yards and is used with hatred to kill an enemy. It is used on one individual at a time. It does not, per se, protect the user from ordinary weapons; rather it makes him a wanted target. It is not a permanent possession, and it is not narrated that Balor ever used it before this battle. As they did not see it they considered that he kept it covered and its victims did not live to tell them.

There were two Mananans, one was a son of Lear and his proper name was Orbision, and Lough Corrib is named from him. He seems to have lost his life when investigating the underground river. The other was the son of Allod, Manánnan Mac Alloid (alloid is the genitive case of allod).

The word 'De' here does not imply divinity though it is translated as Gods. But in early times it is applied to humans who were chiefs or judges or of high rank or possessing outstanding qualities or powers; but always human. We see in sacred scripture where Moses in giving directions to the Israelites about matters to be settled in judgement told them to take the case to the gods; that meant to the judges appointed by whoever was in authority to appoint them.

After their defeat at Telltown they remained a people free and organised, and we read in the beautiful story of four of the

DONEGAL

children of Lir (Lear), Aodh, Con, Fiacra and their sister Finuala, that they elected their own king, the Bobh Dearg, and that Lear had forty chariots when visiting him. (There is a hill near Strabane still called Knockavoe, Cnoc an Bhobh Dearg.) He was the elected king.

The four sons of the Daghda were Aongus, Aodh, Cearmad, and Midhir. Midhir is generally known as Midhir of Bri-Leith (in Longford), Aongus as Aongus Og Mac an Daghda. Aodh (ee) and Cearmad are buried at Cruachan.

In 2738 AM, after the death of his brother Heber Finn Eiremhon became sole monarch and reigned for fourteen years. In his second year as Ard-ri (ree) the nine rivers of Eile broke out, and the three streams of Ua Niolliolo began to flow, and the year he died and was buried at Rathbay on the Nore, the river Eithne broke out and began to flow between Dal na Ruidhe and Dal Riada.

His three sons reigned peacefully together for three years till Muimhne died at Magh Cruachain and Luighne and Laighne fell in Battle of Ard Ladhran fighting the sons of Heber Finn who ruled for a year till they were slain by Irial. Their names were Er, Orbha, Fearan and Feargna.

In 2756 AM, Irial (Faidh, the prophet) son of Eiremhon was learned and could foretell things. He fought because these had basely taken the lives of two of his elder brothers. During his ten years reigning fourteen places were cleared for pasture and crop, namely Magh Reidhchiodh (Morett near Great Heath Portlaoise), Magh Comair (confluence of Boyne and Blackwater), Magh Feile, Magh Sanuis (Connacht), Magh Ninis (in Ulster), Magh Midhe, Magh Luigne (Connacht), Magh Teachta (in Ui Mac Uais), Magh Fearnmhuigne (at Oirghialladh), Magh Cobha (coa at Ui Beathach), Magh Cumaoi (at Ui Neill), Magh Cuile Feadha, Magh Riada and Magh Nairbhrioch (at Fothartuathaibh Airbhrioch in Leinster). He built Rath Ciombaoith at Nemhuin (Navan Fort), Rath Coincheada (near Larne), Rath Mothuigh (at Deag Carbad in Parish of Ryemothey), Rath Buirioch (at Sleachtaibh, County Donegal), Rath Luachat (at Glas Carn), Rath Croicne (Magh Inis, Lecale Co. Down), and Rath Boachoill (at Latharna).

The year after these seven were erected, the three Finn Rivers in Ulster broke out and began to flow, and the next year he won the Battle of Ard Inmath (Teffy) in which Stirne son of Dubh, son of Fomhoir was slain, also the Battle of Teanmhuighe in which Eichtghe leader of the Fomhoraic pirates fell, also the Battle of Loch Muighe in which Lugrot son of Moghfeibhis was slain; also the Battle of Cuill Martho where he overcame the four sons of Heber Finn. In the second year after this, Irial died at Magh Muagh, where he was buried. He was succeeded by his son.

In 2766 AM Eithrial wrote with his own hand the history and travels of the Gaels. Seven woody plains were cut to make land – Tean Mhagh in Connacht, Magh Liogat, Magh Bealaigh at Ui Turatire, Magh Geisile at Ui Failge, Magh Ochtair in Leinster, Lochmhagh in Connacht and Magh Rath at Ui Eachach. He fell in the Battle of Soirrean in Leinster at the hands of Conmaol, a son of Heber Finn, after a reign of wisdom and prudence of twenty years.

In 2786 AM Conmaol succeeded but had to fight many battles against the line of Eiremhon: Ucha, Conucha, Sliabh Beatha, Geisille, wherein Palpa, a son of Eiremhon was slain, Mudhuirn, where Samhro son of Ionbhotha was killed, Lochlein, in which Magrot was slain, Beirre and Aonach Macha, where Conmaol was slain by Heber son of Tighearnmhas.

After the battle he was buried on the south side of Aonach Macha in a place called Feart Chonmaol (grave of Conmaol). He had reigned thirty years.

In 2816 AM he was succeeded by Tighearnmhas, son of Follain, son of Eithrial who reigned for fifty years but fought therein twenty-seven battles against the race of Heber Finn. We give some of their names: Eille (Ely) where Rochorb son of Guillain fell, Comair, Magh Teacht, Loch Moighe, in which Deighiarne, son of Goill, son of Gullain was killed, Cuillard at Moigh Inis, Cuill Fraochan, Ath Ghuirt in Seimhne (Shave-ne), Ard Niadh in Connacht, Carn Fearradhoigh, where Fearradhoch, son of Rochorb, son of Gullain was slain, Cluan Cuis in Teabhtha (Clongows), Comhnuidhe at Tuath Eibhe, Cluan Muireag (north of Breifne), Cuill Faibhair at Earbus (Clare, Co. Galway), seven Battles of Luglocht by Loch Lughach, two battles of Cuill at

Airgead Ross and Reibh, where most of Heber Finn's race was destroyed by the forces of Tighearnmhas.

The following year nine streams broke out of the earth and began to flow namely: Loch Cea, which covered the Plain of Magh Falchuir (Magh Sulchair) near Boyle, Loch Nualline in Connacht, Lochan Iarn in Meath, Lochan Uair, Loch Saighlen, Loch Gabhair (now dry in Co. Meath), Loch Feabhuil at Tir Eoghain, which drowned the district of Feabhuil son of Loduin and Magh Fuinsighe, Dubh Loch at Ard Cianachta, and Loch Dabhuil in Oirghialladh. About this time the Fobhna, Toronn, and Callon black rivers began – perhaps from contact with coal.

A gold mine near Blessington on the Liffey was worked by Iuchadhan (you-huan), and the colours blue and green were invented. The king passed the Ilbreachta Law so that people's rank would be known. A slave's dress was of one colour, soldier's two, a commander's three, a keeper of a house of hospitality four. The nobility five, royalty and the learned six. The Gaels had knowledge of the God of Noah and Israel but this king introduced the worship of more than one god, erected altars and statues and idols and was slain by lightning with three-quarters or two-thirds of his people on the eve of the feast of All Saints as he was worshipping his idol Crom Cruaidh (same as Zoroaster adored in Greece) in Magh Sleachta, Co. Cavan (see 'Saint Patrick after the ancient/narrations').

In 2866 AM Eochaidh Eadgothach son of Daire, son of Conghal, son of Eadamhuin, son of Mail, son of Lughaidh, son of Ith, son of Breogan, held the throne for four years till slain by Cearmna.

In 2870 AM Cearmna and his brother Sobhairce, sons of Eibhric, Heber, Ir and Golamh, divided Ireland between Invir Colpa (mouth of Boyne) and Limerick. Sobhairce erected Dun Sobhairce (three miles east of the Giant's Causeway), and Cearmna erected his castle on the old Head of Kinsale (Dun Mhic Phadraig).

Sobhairce was killed by Eochaidh Meann, son of the king of the Fomhoraic, and Cearmna was slain in the Battle of Dun Cearmna by Eochaidh after a reign of forty years and was succeeded by him.

In 2910 AM Eochaidh Faobharglas son of Conmaol, son of Heber Finn, reigned twenty years. His historical identification name comes from the colour of his well-tempered sword and his two javelins (faobhar = sharp-edged). He reduced part of Alba and made it tributary to the king of Ireland for the Picts had bound themselves by oath to pay homage to the king of Ireland in Eirehon's time, but broke out in frequent rebellion and gave great disturbance to the Irish government. He won the battles of Luachair Deaghadh (in Desmond), Fosuighe da Ghort, The Meeting of the Three Streams, Tuam Dreogan at Breifne, and the Battle of Drum Liathain, over the posterity of Eiremhon. He had seven woods cut down: Magh Smearthain in Ui Faile, one in Magh Laighne in Connacht, Magh Luirg (also in Connacht), Magh Leamhna and Magh Da Gabhal (both in Oirghialladh), Maghan Ionair, Magh Fubhna (Co. Tyrone – Oona water). He was killed in the Battle of Corman by Fiachadh Labhruinne, son of Smiorgioill, son of Eanbothadh, son of king Tighearnmhas, who succeeded and held the throne for twenty-four years. In his time the Inbhir Labhruinne began to flow. The Inbhir Fleisge and Inbhir Maige broke out. Loch Eirne broke out over Magh Geanuinn and drowned many of the Ernai of Magh Ithe. He had a son called Aongus Ollbuadhach (all victorious) who made the Picts, Britons of Alba and the Alban Gaels pay a yearly tribute to Ireland. These Gaels had no tribute to pay until then. Fiachadh fought the descendants of Heber Finn in the battles of Fairge, Galluig, Claire, and Bealgadan, but in this last he was slain by Eochaidh Mumho (Moo-u).

In 2954 AM Eochaidh Mumho reigned for twenty-two years. He was a son of Mofeibhis, Eochaidh Faobharglas, son of Conmaol of Heber Finn's line. He was slain in the Battle of Cliach by Aongus Ollmucach, son of Fiachadh Labhruinne (Eiremhon's line) who held the throne for eighteen years. He was identified from other Aonguses by the historians because he had or he introduced a very good breed of pigs much larger than the native type. He fought the battles of Cleire, Sliabh Cailge where Baiscionn was slain, Moigein Sgiath in Connacht, Glaise Fraochain, where Fraochan Faidh (prophet) was killed, and thirty battles against the Picts, the Firbolgs, and the Orcades (Orkney

Islands).

Three lakes began to flow in his time, namely Loch Einbheithe in Oriel, Loch Failcheadain, and Loch Gasain in Moigh Luirg. He had seven plains cleared of wood and opened up for use, namely Magh Glinne Dearcon in the Cinel Conail's territory, Magh Nionsciach in Leinster, Magh Cuille Caol in Boghuine in Tyrconnell, Aolmhagh at Callroighe, (Drumahaire, Co. Leitrim), Magh Mucruimhe, Magh Luachradh Deaghadh and Magh Archuill in Kerry-Cuachradh. He was slain in the Battle of Carman by Eana Firtheach son of Neachtain.

In 2993 AM Eadna Airgtheach son of Eochaidh Mumho (Heber Finn's line) succeeded for twenty-seven years. He gave shields and targets made of silver to those who excelled in military exploits and without any partiality. He was unfortunately killed by Rotheachta in the Battle of Raighne.

In 3020 AM Rotheachta son of Maoin, son of Aongus Ollmucach succeeded and reigned twenty-five years (Eiremhon's line).

Seadhna slew him and reigned five years. He was son of Artri, Eibhric, Heber, Ir, son of Golamh. He was unfortunately slain by his own son at Cruachan when pirates came there (on mistaking him for a pirate, he had tried on the coat of a pirate).

His son, Fiachadh Fionnsgothach, reigned twenty years. In his time a drink was made from white flowers which were squeezed into cups and used medicinally for many ills. He was killed and succeeded by Muineamhon, son of Cas Clothach, Fear Arda, Rotheachta, Rosa, Glas, Nuaghatt, Eochaidh Faobharglas and Conmoal of the Heber Finn line. He reigned five years. He decreed that gentlemen should wear a chain around their necks. He had a number of helmets with neck and forepiece made of gold in crescent shape made and he bestowed these on his best military men. He is the author of the Golden Chain Knights (a sample of the gold forepiece weighs two ounces). He died of the plague at Magh Aidne. His son succeeded.

In 3075 AM Aildergoid reigned for seven years. He introduced the wearing of gold rings by persons who were very excellent in knowledge or in arts or in sciences or were of great merit. He was killed in the Battle of Teamhuir by Ollamh Fodla son of Fiachadh

HISTORIANS

Fionnsgothach, son of Seadhna (shanna), Artri, Eibhric, Heber, Ir and Golamh of Spain. His reign lasted thirty happy years for he was very learned and of strict virtue. He passed very useful laws for governors and governed, and transmitted to his people a very correct history of the travels, voyages, adventures and wars of the Gaels and the memorable transactions of his own royal family and their names back as far as Fenius Fear Saidh the king of Scuitia. Every third year he summoned the nobility, the draoi, the poets-bards (eigise) and those dealing with history to meet him at Tara to examine or to change or alter the laws where necessary, and to transact any necessary or useful business to advance the honour of his country. This meeting was called the Feis Teamhrach. The chronicles and ancient records were taken care of and what was approved as true of recent time added. Truth in the records was very highly esteemed, fostered and protected by severe sanctions if any historian or bard taught or wrote what was false in the eyes of the learned experts. Experts in the arts and professions were also assembled. If anyone had tried to pervert facts or to give them a biased slant or by a fanciful invention falsify them he was degraded and dismissed with infamy from the bardic assembly for ever. He was liable to be fined, jailed or sentenced appropriately by the competent authority, which was disaster for him. Ollamh is Gaelic for much learning.

The members took their place according to nobility of rank and title, and seats were arranged for the military commanders. It became law that any violence or robbery at this Feis was punished by death, there and then, with no possibility of reprieve. It became the custom for members to assemble six days before business began. This was festive time, and took place three days before till three days after Samhain (Feast of All Saints). Death without the possibility of reprieve was decreed for rape, and the king saw fit to give up his prerogative to grant this type of criminal mercy.

> At Feis of Tara where the learned met
> That goodly laws great Erin get,
> The king was seated on a royal throne,

> And in his face majestic greatness shone,
> A monarch for heroic deeds designed;
> For noble acts become a noble mind.

He also decreed that the dignity of poet, antiquary, physician and harp player should only be conferred on persons of the most illustrious families.

The hall of meeting was long and not wide, a table went down the centre. Things began with a feast. When the dinner was on the table the trumpeter gave a trumpet sound. Then all the shield-bearers came to the door and gave their master's shield to the grand marshall who hung them on the wall on the right side of the table where the princes and nobility were to sit. At the second blast the target-bearers of the generals and of the commanders delivered the targets and they were hung on the wall on the left. At the third blast all came in and took their proper places where they saw their shields or targets which had their proper coat of arms on them. One end of the table was reserved for the learned, the other for the officers of the court. The matter of debate had to be kept secret. No woman was ever to be admitted.

When dinner was over the records were brought and read and examined, and anything that did not concord with fact was erased and only what was judged true and perfect was ordered to be transmitted into the Psalter of Tara, and everything that contradicted what was written in it was deemed of no authority. In the intervals that came between the meetings the nobility and the men of learning collected and submitted for scrutiny the memorable genealogies and events since the last meeting. The pedigrees and the genealogies were strictly preserved. Up to this king's time the common banner of the Gaels had on it a dead serpent and the rod of Moses in memory of Gael's cure, but he decreed that every nobleman and great officer should have his own coat of arms assigned to him by the learned. When he died he was succeeded by hereditary right by his son, who reigned fifteen years.

In 3113 AM Fionnachta reigned, in whose time a great amount of snow fell one year and covered Ireland for a long while. As it thawed it was wine-coloured (perhaps from red arctic dust.) He died and was buried at Magh Inis (Co. Down).

Slanoll his brother reigned fifteen years after him. Slan is Gaelic for health and oll means great. In his reign the people remained healthy, very few got sick or died of any malignant disease. He died in the Teach Miodcuarta of an unknown cause. He was succeeded by Geide Ollguthach, his brother, who reigned seventeen years. (Oll = great, Guth = voice, perhaps some deafness was in high places). He was killed by Fiachadh, son of Fionnachta, who reigned twenty years and four more that were disputed. Bearngall, son of Geide succeeded, and reigned twelve years till killed by Oilioll, son of Slanoll, who reigned sixteen years till killed by Siorna Saolach.

In 3212 AM Siorna Saolach son of Dein, Rotheachta, Maoin, Aongus Ollmucach, of Eiremhon's line took the throne. Saolach means long lived. His reign lasted twenty-one years but he had reached a great age when slain at Aillin by Rotheachta son of Roan, Failbhe, Cas Cead Caingniodh, Aildergoid, Muineamhoin, Cas Clothach, Firarda, Rotheachta, Rosa, Glas, Nuaghatt Deaghlamh, Eochaidh Faobharglas, Conmaol (Prince of Chiefs), son of Heber Fionn.

He perished by fire at Dun Sobhairce after a reign of seven years and was succeeded by Elim, son of Rotheachta, son of Roan, who was slain after one year by Giallacha, son of Oliolla Olchaoin, son of Siorna Saoghalach who was king for nine years, till killed at Moighe Muadh by Art Imleach.

Art Imleach, son of Elim, reigned twenty-two years till killed by Nuadha Fionn Fail, son of Giallacha (line of Eiremhon) who also reigned twenty years, till slain by Breasrigh, son of Art Imleach (Heber Fionn's line) who reigned nine years and fought many battles against pirates who infested our coasts. He was killed at Carn Cluain by Eochaidh Apthach, son of Fin, Oliolla, Floinruadh, Roithlain, Martineadh, Sithchin, Riaglan, Eochaidh Breac, Luigheach and Ith, son of Breogan. Apthach denotes infection or a plague. He reigned one year and during that year a malignant disease that they could not cure infected the whole people every month bringing great mortality.

In 3302 AM Eochaidh Apthach was killed by Fionn, son of Bratha, son of Labhraidh, son of Cairbre, son of Ollamh Fodla,

Found in surface clay in Mongavlin, Co. Donegal. On right is a human head with beard. On left is the backbone view of an animal not yet identified.

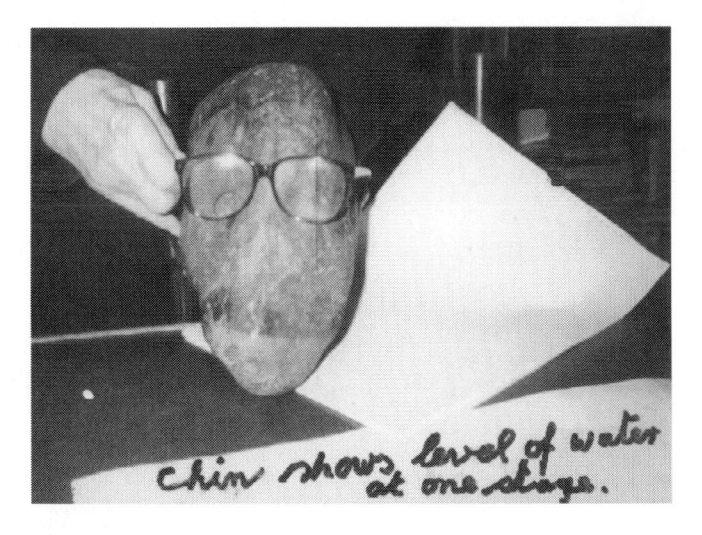

Example of a petrified male human head. Note the external colouring around the chin, caused by the stagnant water of the eiscir. This indicates clearly the angle this head was lying at in the eiscir.

We have many examples of human petrification of parts of the human anatomy. It is easier to discern heads than, for example, pieces of leg, arm and interior organs such as hearts, eyes et cetera, which were in many cases petrified on their own. In this case we have a child's head petrified and showing disfiguration around the mouth. The back of this example is hollow and made up of red clay which we presume is the result of the imperfect petrification of organisms. Yes, lots of children perished in the global flood.

This is a petrified right hind foot of a horse: a blacksmith volunteered to make a shoe for it and the measurement he took was 6.5 inches by 6.5 inches. He recognised it instantly as a horse's foot.

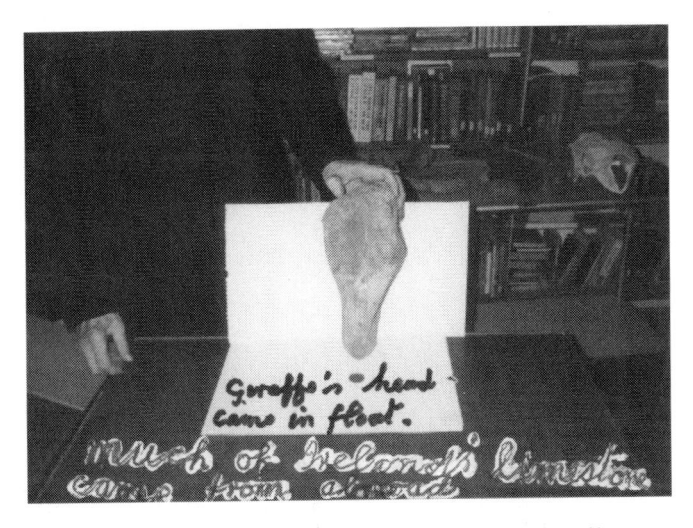

A petrified giraffe's head. Many carcasses came in the float. The amount of limestone in Ireland increased dramatically as a result of the flood. Allow for distortion.

Three petrified heads. Evolution is an erroneous theory floated on mythical geology and on mythical time. Only historical geology is tenable.

Petrified body of female human showing where the head broke off and a garment on the left arm with a three-plaited belt. Also a large head to left of picture.

Sea stack off Mayo coast. Formed by over forty tides of the Sea of Deluge (which later took away its surroundings). Two layers and two divisions per day built it up in about eight weeks, but it took many hundreds of years to isolate it.

who reigned twenty years till slain by Seadhna Ionaraicc who also reigned twenty years. He was son of Breasrigh, son of Art Imleach (of the Heber Fionn line). He was the first to settle a constant pay for his officers and soldiers. He instituted a form of military discipline that remained for many centuries. He died in dreadful torment by having his limbs pulled out by Simon Breac, who took the crown. He was son of Nuadh Fionn Fail (line of Eiremhon) and reigned six years till he was seized by Duach Fionn, who punished him with the same kind of torture as he had inflicted on Duach's father Seadhna (there is a place called Carnshanna near the White Cross east of Raphoe).

In 3348 AM Duach Fionn was on the throne five years till slain by Muireadhach Bolgrach son of Simon Breac, who was king for four years and then was killed by Eadna (ae-na) Dearg a son of Duach Fionn. (North of Carnshanna there is Mondooey, Castledoey Carraigballadooey and Dooey's hill.)

In 3357 AM Eadna Dearg, son of Duach Fionn, son of Seadhna Ionaraicc (ionaraic = wages) wore the crown for twelve years. He was remarkable for his red complexion. He had a mint erected and coined money at Airgiodross. He died at Sliabh Mis where he was buried, smitten by a plaque that depopulated much of Ireland.

Lughaidh Iardhonn, his son, succeeded and reigned nine years. (Iardhonn = dark brown hair). He was killed at Raith Clochair by and succeeded by Siorlamh son of Fionn, Breatha, Labhra, Cairbre, Ollamh Fodla (Ir's line), and he reigned sixteen years. (Sior = long, lamh = hand.) His arms were so long that he could touch the ground with his fingers when standing. He was slain by Eochaidh Uaircheas who seized the crown and ruled twelve years. He was a son of Lughaidh Iardhonn. He got the name Uaircheas from his invention of curachs made of skins which he used during his two years of banishment as landing craft to plunder the coasts from the thirty ships that he had. He was slain by Eochaidh Fiadhmhuine and his brother Conuing Begaglach sons of Duach Teamhrach, Muireadhach Bolgrach, Simon Breac of the line of Eiremhon, and they reigned together five years, but lost the throne when Eochaidh was slain by Lughaidh Lamhdhearg. (Fiadh = deer, muine = thicket; he was fond of hunting.)

In 3411 AM Lughaidh Lamhdhearg had a red spot on one

hand. He was a son of Eochaidh Uaircheas (Heber Fionn's line). He reigned seven years till he was killed by Conning Begaglach. He was seen to be fearless (beg = little, eagla = fear). He resumed the government and reigned ten years. He had a strong constitution and a mind capable of designing and carrying out great things. He fought successfully against the country's enemies, he governed with justice and with moderation and was well-loved by his subjects, but he was slain by Art, son of Lughaidh Lamhdhearg, who governed six years, but fell by the hand of Duach Laghrach, assisted by Duach's father, Fiachaidh Tolgrach.

In 3434 AM Fiachaidh Tolgrach son of Muireadhach Balgrach, son of Simon Breac (of Eiremhon's line) reigned seven years but fell by Oilill Fionn son of Art (Heber's line) who reigned nine years till killed by Airgeadmhar, and by Fiachaidh and Duach, son of Fiachaidh.

In 3450 AM Eochaidh son of Oilioll Fionn, son of Art (Heber's line) succeeded for seven years till slain at a meeting by Duach Laghrach with whom he had made peace and with whose aid he withstood Airgeadmhar, giving him no place in the government.

Airgeadmhar son of Siorlamh, Fionn, Bratha, et cetera (Ir's line) succeeded and reigned twenty-three years till killed by Duach Laghrach and Lughaidh Laighdhe. He was succeeded by Duach Laghrach, who held the throne for ten years. He was strict and hasty in punishing criminals. He was a son of Fiachaidh Tolgrach.

In 3490 AM Lughaidh Laighdhe, having slain Duach Laghrach, ascended the highly desired throne of Ireland. He held it for seven years. He was son of Eochaidh, son of Oilioll Fionn (Heber's line). There were five Lughaidhs in that family – a draoi had foretold that his son Lughaidh would be king but his father Eochaidh Daire Domhtheach (of the time of famine) was not told which, so he named them all Lughaidh and in time asked the draoi which. He was told the next day at the convention of Tailtean, where he was to take his sons, that a young deer running would be seen by him and that the whole company would run after it and the Lughaidh who would catch it would be king. At Beann Eadair a druidical mist separated the brothers from the rest of the pursuers and they followed it to Dail Maschorb were

Lughaidh Laighde overtook and killed it (Laighde = fawn).

He had great difficulty in getting the throne, but having seen Ireland as a very old woman, whom he embraced, she turned into a beautiful young lady and he was rewarded for all his pains by becoming the king and the possessor of one of the most fruitful and desirable islands in the world for seven years till slain by Aodh Ruadh, son of Badhorn, Airgeadmhar, Siorlamh, Fionn, Bratha, Labhraidh, Cairbre and Ollamh Fodla (of Ir's line) who reigned twenty-one years till drowned at Eas Aodha Ruaidh (eas = waterfall) on the Earne.

In 3518 AM Diothorba son of Deaman, Airgeadmhar and Siorlamh of the line of Ir, son of Golamh, succeeded and reigned twenty-one years till killed by the three Cuans at Corann.

In 3539 AM Ciombaoth son of Fionntan, son of Airgeadmhar next took the throne and reigned twenty years till he died by a plague at Eomhain Mhacha.

In 3559 AM Macha Mongruadh (red-haired) claimed the throne as the only heir of Aodh Ruadh when it became her father's turn to rule for Aodh, Ciombaoth and Diothorba had agreed, when tired of fighting, to reign in turn for twenty-one years, and the turn had come round for Aodh to reign again, so she claimed it was her father's turn and she was his heir. But Diothorba would not hear of a woman ruling the warlike Gaels. She gathered her loyal followers and defeated Diothorba and his five sons and their forces. Their names were Baoth, Buadhach, Bras, Uallach and Borbchas. Her victory was complete, but they tried again and in a desperate battle she won again, and the brothers fled, and their father soon died in great grief. Macha married Ciombaoth. She captured the brothers and refused to put them to death, though requested to do so. She insisted that it would be contrary to laws and customs of the country to execute them but that instead their punishment might be to erect a royal palace where the royal court would be. They agreed to this, considering it just, and the queen drew out with her neck-pin (that was for keeping her hair in place) the plan of the structure which became known after that as Eomhain Mhacha (eo = pin, muin = neck). It is about two miles west of Armagh and is now called Navan Fort.

She was strong, robust and active and able to endure hardships. She governed in a magnificent manner which delighted her subjects and quietened any potential enemy, but she was at last slain by Reachta Righdhearg son of Lughaidh Laighde (of Heber's line). He held the throne for twenty years. He had a very red arm. He has been called Monarch of Ireland and Alba, for he had sent an army into Alba under the two sons of Irial Glunmhuir, Ferc and Iboth, who subdued the Picts (Cruithnigh) to keep them tributary. He was slain by Ughaine Mor.

In 3586 AM Ughaine Mor, son of Eochaidh Buadhach, son of Duach Laghrach (of Eiremhon's line) reigned thirty years. Ughaine Mor had been fostered by Macha and that was why he killed Reachta for fosterage brought about a very close bond of friendship. He married Ceasar Cruthach, daughter of the king of France. He also made the Picts pay tribute. He got ready a mighty fleet and sailed into the Mediterranean, landed in Africa and from there went to Sicily and other islands and was called Monarch of Ireland, Alba and of all the western islands of Europe. He had twenty-two sons and three daughters, and he divided Ireland between these twenty-five. By these divisions the taxes were collected for about three hundred years. He was slain by his brother Badhbhchadh (bove-hoo) who reigned a day and a half till he was slain inhumanly by a son of Ughaine at Teallach an Coscair (near Gormanstown). He took the throne.

Laoghaire Lorc reigned two years (Lorc = slaughter or murder). His brother, to whom he showed great kindness, envied him and so desired to be king of Ireland that he pined away and became thin. Only the kingdom would content him. He was near death and Laoghaire visited him but he asked him not to bring a bodyguard next time for it looked as if he did not trust him, and Laoghaire did so, having assured him he did not distrust him, but had the armed retinue for the purpose of maintaining royal dignity and that he would not bring them next time. The sick man determined to treacherously kill his unarmed brother and took counsel of an unworthy draoi who advised him to pretend to be dead and have a dagger hidden and when he leant over the bier to stab him. He did this, and had also his son Oillill Aine slain to secure the succession, and so tortured Oillill's young son that he lost the power of speech and was left alive for as this was a blemish he could not be Ard-ri. His friends had him taken to South Munster where he recovered his speech when hit by a hurly. He was sent to France to his relatives so they gave him only nine in his retinue.

Cobhthach Caol mBreagh (caol = thin, Breagh, the plain in which he lay sick) ruled peacefully for thirty years till killed by Maon.

In 3648 AM Maon succeeded for eighteen years. In France at the age of twenty-five (or somewhat before it) he showed such ability that the king gave him supreme command of his troops. The daughter of Scoriat, his Munster foster-father sent him presents and a song of praise (amhra) by the bard Craftine, and instructed him to play tunes and sing the amhra to him. It expressed her attitude towards him and encouraged him to come back to Erin and assert his right. Her name was Moriat. His friendly and trustworthy persons at court so impressed the king with the justice of his cause that he approved and gave him twenty-two hundred troops and sufficient ships. He called by Alba and afterwards landed at Wexford, went quickly to Dinn Riogh, destroyed the murderer and thirty of the princes, and took the throne.

'Who is the hero who has done this?'

'It is Loingseach.'

'Is he able to speak?' asked a draoi.

'He is,' was the satisfying answer.

(Labhair is the verb to speak and from that the historians called him Labhradh and Loingseach from his being admiral of the fleet (luingios = fleet).

When he had things fixed up to his satisfaction he took Craftine south and he was very well received by Moriat's father, and soon she became Queen of Ireland.

Labhradh Loingseach reigned eighteen years. As his ears were rather large he kept them covered with his hair. He introduced Gaulish spears into the Province of Leinster which takes its name from them (laighne is a spear). They were broad and called Glas - in colour. This might be their colour if a grinding stone was used to finish them while still hot. The chief families of Leinster (except O'Nolan) are descended from Labhradh. These are the families descended from Labhradh: O'Connor, Cavanagh, Murphy, O'Toole, O'Branain, Fitzpatrick, O'Duinn, O'Dempsey, O'Dwyre and O'Ryan. O'Nolan is from Cobhthach. Labhradh is said to be learned and brave. He was slain by Meilge Molbhthach (Moluagh), a son of this Cobhthach, and he reigned seven years and was killed by Modhcorb, son of (another) Cobhthach Caomh (beautiful) son of Reachta Righdearg (Heber's line). He reigned also seven years, but was slain by Aongus Ollamh, who reigned eighteen years. This king was learned and was a son of Oiliolla and a grandson of Labhradh Loingseach (Eiremhon's line). He fell by Iarainnghleo Fathach (the wise) son of Meilge. He was studious and of good judgement and reigned seven years till he fell by Fearchorb, son of Modhchorb of Heber's line, who reigned eleven years till slain by Conla Cruaidh Cealgach, (cruaidh = hard, cealg = sting), a son of Iarainngleo. He reigned four years and it is not now known how he died. He was succeeded by his son.

In 3720 AM Oiliolla Caisfhiachlach reigned twenty-five years till slain at Tara by Adamhar Foltchaoin (fair-haired) son of Fearchorb, and he reigned five years.

He was slain by Eochaidh Foltleathan who reigned eleven years (folt = hair, leathan = wide) son of Oiliolla of the line of Eiremhon. He was slain by Feargus Fortamhuill, who reigned twelve years, son of Breasal Breac, Aongus Gailine, Oiliolla Bracain, Labhradh Loingseach. He had great strength and was very brave but fell by the sword of Aongus Tuirmheach.

In 3773 AM Aongus Tuirmheach, son of Eochaidh Foltleathan reigned thirty years. He avoided being seen in public for when intoxicated he had violated his daughter and was very much ashamed at what he had done (Tuirmheach = ashamed). A son resulted and the child was taken to a boat and abandoned on the sea. The boat was furnished with very rich clothes and utensils and riches to defray the expenses of rearing and educating him and it was soon found by fishermen who got a nurse for him and looked after him well, knowing he was a son of rich people, and they called him Fiachadh. He was known to the historians as Fiachadh Fearmara (of the sea). Aongus had a legitimate son well before this and he is the ancestor of the Siol Cuinn in general. Aongus was slain at Tara by the sword.

Conall, known as Callamhrach, son of Eidirsgeoil, son of Eochaidh Foltleathan of the line of Eiremhon succeeded and reigned five years. He was killed by Niadh Seadhamhuin, son of Adhamhar Foltchaoin, who reigned seven years; Heber Finn's line. His mother Fleidhis was able to cause the wild hinds to allow themselves to be milked as if tame. She was described as a sorceress.

Niadh was slain by Eanna Aighneach, son of Aongus Tuirmheach, son of Eochaidh Foltleathan and he reigned twenty-eight years. He was liberal, free and hospitable, and gave many gifts. He was slain by Criomhthan Cosgrach, son of Feidlim-Foirtruin, Feargus Fortamhail, Breasal Breac, of Eiremhon's line, who reigned seven years and was very brave at the head of his army and always victorious. He was killed in 3850 AM by Rughraidhe son of Sithrighe, Dubh, Fomhar, Airgeadmhar and Siorlamh (of Ir's line) and held the throne for thirty years, but may have reigned as a lesser king for forty years before that. He died a natural death at Airgidross and was succeeded by Ionadhmhar, son of Niadh Seadhamhuin of Heber's line, who reigned three years till slain by Breasal Bodhiabha, son of Rughraidhe. During his reign of eleven years a cattle disease raged and killed most of the cows and black cattle all over Ireland. He was killed by Lughaidh Luaghne son of Ionadhmhar of Heber's line and he ruled for five years but was slain by Congall Claringneach son of Rughraidhe, who reigned thirteen years but fell by Duach Dallta Deaghaidh.

In 3912 AM Duach Dallta Deaghaidh, son of Cairbre Luiscleathan, son of Lughaidh Luaghne of Heber Fionn's line, reigned ten years. He had a younger brother who was equally brave in warrior exploits but who secretly raised an army to take the throne. Duach got word of this and invited him to court, seized him and took out his eyes so as to blemish him and thereby to make him unfit to reign. After this Duach looked after him with great care in a very brotherly way and with great generosity. Deaghadh was his name. The historians, because he was a good foster-father to him, identified him by the name Duach Dallta

Deaghaidh. The Earnai came to Munster in his time.

He was slain by and succeeded by Fachtna Fathach son of Cas, Rughraidhe, Sithrighe, et cetera, and reigned eighteen years. He was well educated, was wise and possessed many accomplishments and made useful laws and governed with prudence and moderation till slain by Eochaidh Feiliach.

In 3940 AM Eochaidh Feiliach son of Fionn, Finlogha, Roighnean Ruadh, Easamhuin Eamhna, Blathachta, Labhraidh Loirc, Eanna Aighneach, of the line of Eiremhon succeeded and reigned twelve years. He lost his triplet sons in the Battle of Dromchriadh and till his death lamented for them in a sighing sort of manner. Their names were Breas, Nar and Lothar. Their mother's name was Cloithfhionn, daughter of Eochaidh Uchtleathan, who is described as a very virtuous lady and the boy princes as boys of great promise. Eithne, the mother of Deaghaidh (called by historians Eithne Gubha-Eithne the sorrowful), mourned till her death his being blinded.

Eochaidh arranged Ireland into five provinces: Ulster, Leinster, Connacht and two Munsters. Feargus, son of Leighe got Ulster, Leinster went to Rossa, son of Feargus Fairge. He divided Connacht into three parts between Fiodhach son of Feig and the two sons of Connraidh: Eochaidh Allat and Tinne. He gave one part of Munster to a son of Luchta. Tighearnach Teadhbheamach and the other to one of his own line whom he treated with great affection but who had been put out of his territory around Loch Eirne by the Clanna Rudhruidhe and driven south with the Ernai. His name was Deaghadh, son of Suin, son of Oilill Earna, son of Fiachadh Fear Mara. He acted so prudently and well that he was elected king of the two divisions of Munster.

Eochaidh gave Tinne his own daughter Maeve in marriage for when asked he offered him any place to build a Palace, but the other two refused and Tinne was well rewarded and was made Prime Minister. The draoi were asked where would be the best place and they said Drom na nDruagh. The best architect drew up the plans, and the ditch to surround the pile was finished in one day. Maeve called the rath Rath Cruachain. It was the Domhanraidh who were called on to make and shape the rampart but they got no pay for this great day's work. Eochaidh made his son-in-law king of Connacht but he was killed at Tara by Monuidhir. After that she married Oillioll Mor, son of Rossa Ruadh, a Leinster man whose mother, Matha Muireag, was a Connacht woman and he was born in Connacht. Maeve became the mother of the seven Maine. A Northern warrior ran him through with a lance at Cruachan and the Connacht people, who esteemed him greatly, pursued Conal Cearnach hotly and killed him. Eochaidh kept the Province of Meath (named from Midhe, a son of Bratha, Breogan's father) to be always for the Ard-ri; and he died a natural death.

When Maeve was in her second widowhood the long war between her and Ulster took place. At the birth of Deirdre of the sorrows the draoi Cathbhadh (caf-oo) foretold she would bring or occasion great misfortune and loss to Ulster. Some wanted her killed immediately but King Connor son of Fachtna Fathach (he was called Connor Mac Nessa from his mother Nessa) would not allow it, but had her nursed and kept strictly and intended to marry her. She eloped with Naoise, one of the sons of Uisneach. They went to Alba but, later, Connor agreed to let them back, for they were in dire straits. On their return he had them treacherously killed, so a number of the Red Branch Knights joined Maeve and the men of Ulster came off badly. The war stopped when Maeve was hit by a stone from the sling of Ferbhuidhe son of Connor, eight years after the death of Oilioll Mor. About a year after Naoise's death Deidre was still so inconsolable that Connor gave up hope and gave her to Eoghan who had killed her husband but after a remark by Connor, with Eoghan in the Chariot, that she was like a ewe between two rams, she leaped out of the chariot and split her skull. She had neither looked up nor smiled since widowed.

King Connor's young nephew, Setanta, being also invited to a feast by the armourer, Cualan, would not come until he finished a game of hurley. He arrived when the doors were closed and the guard dog would not let him in so he killed it and after that he had to do guard himself, until another dog was got. He became known then as Cu-Chuailin – the hound of Cualan – the armourer (cu = hound). It sadly happened that Cuchuailin came face to face with his bosom friend, Ferdia, and did not want to hurt him and told him so. But Ferdia being in Maeve's army had no choice but fight. At the end of the first and second day they gave their arms to their charioteers, who were brothers, and they embraced each other and sent a share of their ointments and healing herbs and food to each other, but not so the third night, and on the fourth day Ferdia pressed the fight so hard that Cuchuailin, to save himself, had to strike a mortal wound and Ferdia died from it. The place is called Ardee (ath = ford, Fherdia = Ferdia). Cuchuailin swooned but soon recovered, helped by Laogh his charioteer. He was badly wounded.

Conal Cearnach figures in the defence of Ulster and once a Connacht champion raided Ulster, killed three warriors of the Red Branch in single combat and was on his way back home but was overtaken by Conal at Ath Cheit. Ceat was killed and Conal had swooned. Bealcu Breifne found both and said, 'I'm delighted that you pair of boys have knocked yourselves out at last after having troubled the provinces for so many years.'

'Your remarks are quite insupportable and in other circumstances I would not put up with them. Kill me and it will be said I was killed by two.'

'I'll do no such thing. I'll take you home, get you the best doctor and remedies.'

'Well, I'll fight you when I'm better.'

'All right,' said Bealcu, seeing little prospect for him in the warrior line. Against all expectations he soon got well and Bealcu and his three sons plotted to kill him. Conal got a presentiment of danger, rose from his bed and said, 'Change beds with me.' 'I will not.' 'I'll kill you if you don't.' The three came in, stabbed their father and Conal killed them instantly.

Feargus Mac Roigh, a red branch knight who had joined Maeve was killed by an attendant of Oillioll Mor, Maeve's husband, who cast a spear at him at Oilioll's order. Oilioll thought that his wife Maeve was too fond of Feargus. This Feargus was called Mac Roigh from his mother, with Rossa Ruadh his father. Oillioll's jealousy arose from observing both.

Laoghaire Buadhach lost his life by breaking his skull rushing out of his own door, having hit the lintel when he helped prevent an unworthy poet from being drowned. King Connor had said,

'Drown him,' and Laoighaire's servants said, 'Is there no place else to drown the poet but outside our master's door? We'll not allow it.'

Laoghaire joined the fray with success but as he had hit his head on the lintel of his door rushing out he then dropped dead. (Aodh mac Ainninn was the poet.) The place was beside Loch Laoghaire, now Lough Mary. There is a place called Booey's Ford in the townland of Drummucklagh, Co. Donegal.

Queen Maeve in old age retired to Inis Clothrann in Loch Ribh, and her custom was to bathe every summer morning in the lake. Ferbhuidhe, son of King Connor, found this out and secretly measured the distance from there to the opposite shore. He went home and practised at a target at that distance till he became expert at hitting it with his sling, called cran-Thubal (Thubal was a son of Japheth). Ferbhuidhe came to the east side of the Shannon with an Ulster gathering and one morning he hit her on the head with a pebble and she drowned. She had ruled Connacht eighty-nine years and was buried at Cruachan. She was the mother of triplets: Ciar, Conmac and Corc.

Feargus Mac Roigh was their father. (There is a rock in Greach a' da chuas in East Donegal called Carrick Roy.) From Ciar came the Ciarraidhe (the people of Kerry), from Conmac the Conmaicne of Connacht, and from Corc the name Corca Moruadh (Co. Clare).

King Connor got his death wound by being hit on the skull by a brain ball from the cran-Thubal of Ceat, but he survived for seven years under strict doctor's orders to do nothing that would excite him. The doctor was Fingin Fathach. Connor's death is associated with Good Friday. Conal Cearnach was with him. They saw in a vision a great perturbation of nature and convulsion and falling darkness when they were in the wood of Lamhruaide, and they asked the draoi Bacrach what was the meaning or reason for such. He told them the prehistory of the Lord's crucifixion (the story Bacrach told them in prophetic prehistory that the cause of what they saw was of a barbarous murder of a most innocent and divine person, Jesus Christ, the son of the Everlasting God).

The king cried out that he would be avenged, seeing such villainy by the Jews, who had the insolence to destroy the Lord, the son of the great God of all the earth. He drew his sword and, in fierce anger at the thought of that abominable act, cut and hacked at the trees, saying that if he were there he would chop in pieces the murderers like these trees. The anger and excitement caused the wound in his skull to open and he dropped dead. Bacrach was a Leinster draoi.

There was some difficulty over who was to succeed him, but it was agreed amicably that whoever carried Connor's body to Eomhuin without resting would be the successor – he was heavy. Cronn Bearruidhe, one of his footmen, took it up carried it to the top of Sliabh Fuaid (son of Breogan) and dropped dead, and his name is known in Irish when referring to a person whose ambition leads to his ruin.

Curaoi mac Daire was a famous Munster warrior and was also expert at magic, as we shall see:

> The day was cold the snow lay deep
> That night at Eomhuin Mhacha.
> The warriors sit and vigil keep,
> None drank of Uisge beatha (whiskey).
> The door to inside open flies –
> Wind, snow and man do enter
> Leary Buadhach is chief inside.
> 'Unannounced who does venture?'
>
> 'My name is Uadhach,
> 'I come to seek a man who keeps his word.'
> 'You need not move from where you speak
> 'Our deeds and words concord.'
> 'Very good,' then Uadhach said:
> 'The bargain I seek is this:
> 'Him to cut off tonight my head –
> 'Then me to cut off his.'
>
> Laoghaire made the bargain.
> Leary saw no flaw.
> Uadhach from his armpit
> A hatchet out did draw.

Leary took the hatchet
He never had one so fine,
No other tool to match it,
The best one of its kind.

They got a piece of firewood
Intended for the fire.
On it Uadhach stretched his neck –
The hatchet rises higher.
The deed is done, the head is off,
But when you'd count a score
The body rises, gets its head,
And goes towards the door.

But as it did it there turns round.
The head to Leary spake:
'It will be your turn tomorrow night,'
And Leary's knees did shake.
As was agreed, in he came –
It was the following night.
He looked around but all the same
No Leary was in sight.

But Conal Cearnach was in charge
He is worthy all will grant.
'Who are you?' he asked the man,
'And tell us what you want.'
Conal had been absent,
He hadn't heard a word,
But agreed he'd make the bargain
And then unsheathed his sword.

'Defend yourself,' said Conal.
'Oh, there'll be no defence.
'I'm going to let you do it,'
And Conal's lips went tense.

'All we in here our word do keep.
'Our word you see is our bond.
'But west and south you may find sheep
'Who'll drink at every pond.

'I thought I'd have a joyful fight –
'Some swordplay suits me well.'
Uadhach's neck is severed
After flash of sword he fell.
Conal's knees began to shake
As Uadhach turns at door –
'Tomorrow night,' the head spake
As it spoke the night before.

Word came to King Connor:
Leinster made a raid.
Conal mounts his chariot
And goes to farmers' aid.
He was not back when Uadhach came,
But Cuchuailin then was there
And similar words to him he said,
But Cuchuailin moved with care.

'Will you do this thing yourself
'Or get someone else to do it?'
He wouldn't be cutting heads next night
And well Cuchuailin knew it.
'Oh I myself will do that thing.
'I use no servant boy.'

Out Cuchuailin begins to bring
His sword to it employ.
His eye has viewed the part to strike
And scarce a flash is seen.
Cuchuailin's sword is scarcely stained
That through Uadhach's neck has been.

'Your turn t'will be tomorrow night,'
Says Uadhach's severed head.
Cuchuailin's muscles then get tight...
He knew he'd soon be dead.

In came a man and talk was stilled
Wearing in health his head.
'Here's the man Cuchuailin killed
'By cutting off his head.'
Old Sgeal the historian warrior
At speed to Connor goes.
'Come and save Cuchuailin,
'Our strength against our foes.

'There's a man about to kill him
'By trick and pledged word,
'A man who came to life again
'When killed by hasty sword.'
Mac Nessa reached the Red Branch Hall.
His face was hot and red.
'Is there no way out Cuchuailin?'
'No way,' Cuchuailin said.

'Surely something can be done –
'Otherwise you'll be dead.
'Is there any way out, Setanta?'[1]
'I wish there were,' he said.
Then turning to the stranger,
'What are you waiting for?'
'I won't wait long, no danger
'If your neck that block won't stir.'

Cuchuailin takes position,
But still no blow came down.
In anger, not contrition,
Cuchuailin's head turns round.

---

[1] Young Cuchuailin was called Setanta, and he was a nephew of King Connor.

'What for delay?' Cuchualin said.
'I just was going to see
'If my axe is sharp enough...
'Your sword was sharp,' said he.

He took a hair from out his chin,
On edge he let it fall.
Two halves 'thas parted in.
Uadhach stretches tall,
Like a shadow Uadhach lengthened
To take a mighty stroke,
Whereat the axe struck rafter;
The haft he nearly broke.

Successful was his effort
To get the hatchet free.
He took another stroke at him
And missed by inches three.
'You're the man I'm looking for.
'Your head is where it should be.
'I've found a man who keeps his word.'
And all with him agree.

'A nation that does not keep its word
May expect to not survive.'
(But a good and faithful people
Can always hope to thrive.)
'Good night. I must return at once
'To Southern Dun Conraoi.'
Then all knew this magician
Was Daire's son, Curaoi.

Cuchuailin led a plundering party to an island called Manainn (it was called earlier Mana – Isle of Man) but failed to capture the dun where the riches were. Curaoi had come there, but disguised, wearing grey clothes, and when they were about to return empty-handed he said he would capture it if they would agree to give him whatever jewel he chose. Cuchuailin gave him his word of honour he'd have it, so he used his powers of enchantment to stop a magical wheel that prevented entrance. All were slain except the young, beautiful virgin, Blanaid.

At the dividing of the spoils the man in grey claimed his jewel – Blanaid. 'No,' said Cuchuailin, 'the bargain I made was for a precious stone.' He would not give Blanaid. 'You're not keeping your word now.' But he said firmly that he was not honour-bound to that interpretation of jewel. There was no give on either side so Curaoi soon found his opportunity of taking Blanaid, by his magical powers, from where they were dividing the spoils at Eomhuin Mhacha, and left them with their precious stones.

When it was found she was missing, the search started, but she was not found, so he guessed that Curaoi was the taker and proceeded towards Munster and overtook both at Sulchoid (Co. Tipperary). They fought, but Curaoi won and tied up Cuchuailin, cut off his hair and left him there and set out for his own Riogh Phuirt with Blanaid. However Laogh son of Rian of Gabhra came on the scene and released him. But to avoid the disgrace of having a very unwarrior-like haircut he went and hid in Beanna Boirce (Co. Down) and lived secretly with Laogh for a year till his hair grew. Then one day he saw a large flock of black birds going south-west. He followed them and brought down one in every district with his sling using the method of the taithbheim (tihveim) (return stroke). The last he killed was at Sruibh Broin in West Munster.

Returning, he found Blanaid near her dun, and she asked him to rescue her from one she did not want. He was pleased and she told him she would get Curaoi to build a stronger fort and get him to scatter his men – the Clanna Deaghaidh – to fetch large stones, and told him to come about Samhain (Halloween). He came with the help King Connor gave him and hid and sent her word. He got the reply that he should attack when he would see the stream run white with milk, and that she would steal Curaoi's sword. All worked as planned. Curaoi was killed and the river got the name Fionnglaise (white brook). Firchertne the Poet followed them and found Connor and Cuchuailin with an assembly around them, and finding Blanaid at the edge of the Ceann Beara cliff he grabbed her and threw himself and her to their death. (Co.

Antrim). Curaoi's mother was Morann Manannach, daughter of Ir, son of Uinnsidhe, sister of Eochaidh Eachbheoil.

When Cuchuailin himself was dying of wounds at the Battle of Muirtheimhne he had himself tied upright to a standing stone, sword in hand, his shield raised up and his two spears by his left side in order to still terrify the enemy and to give more courage to his own men. The foe was using infernal powers against him. But a little divine child appeared to him before he died and said, comforting the dying hero, 'Fear them not, my brother, these are children of iniquity, their dominion is but for a time.' An otter came and began to drink his blood.

In 3952 AM Eochaidh Aireamh succeeded Eochaidh Feiliach. He was son of Fionn, Finlogha, Roighnean Ruadh, Easamhuin Eamhna, Blathachta, Labhraidh Loirc, et cetera of Eiremhon's line and he reigned for twelve years. He introduced grave-digging and directed that the head be placed west of the feet and that a leacht be raised over the grave. (A leacht can be a flagstone or a grave mound.) The draoi performed the religious funeral rites, the Poet proclaimed the virtues of the deceased, his bravery, his hospitality and his humour. Later it remained a custom, if passing by, to throw a stone on the leacht and this preserved the cairn. Place names often preserve the name of the person whose grave it is.

He was slain by Siodhmall son of Cairbre Crom and was succeeded by Eidersgoil son of Eogan, Oilioll, Iar, Deagha, Suin, Roisin, Trean, Rothrein, Airindil, Maine, Forga, Fearadhach, Oiliolla Euron and Fiacha Fear Mara of the line of Eiremhon. He has been referred to as 'the good Eidersgoil'.

He reigned for six years, but was killed at Aillin by and succeeded by Nuaghadh Neacht, son of Seadna Siothbhach, Lughaidh Loithfhionn, Breasal Breac, Fiachadh Fiorbric, Oiliolla Glas, Fearaidheach Foghlas, Nuaghat Follamhuin, Alloid, Art, Criomhthan Cosgrach, Fearadhach Fionn, Feilimidh Foirthruin, Feargus Fortamhail, Breasal Breoghaman and Aongus Gailine of Eiremhon's line. He reigned for half a year till slain by Eidersgoil's son Conaire.

Conaire reigned thirty years, and is called Conaire Mor. From him descend the ruling families of the Earnaigh of Munster, who were banished from the Loch Earne territory by the Clana

Rughraidhe; also the Dal Riada of Alba descend from him. He was slain by Aingeal Caol son of the king of the Britains (or Cambria).

In 4000 AM Lughaidh Riabh-dearg then reigned for twenty years, son of one of the Fineamhnas (triplets) grandson of Eoachaidh Feiliach. He married Dearbhorguill, daughter of the king of Denmark. He had a red circle round his neck and another round his body. He fell on his sword upon some discontent and put an end to himself.

Connor Abhradhruadh (red eyebrows) succeeded. He was the son of Feargus Fairge, Nuaghadh Neacht, et cetera of Eiremhon's line and reigned one year. The Lia Fail is silent from his time. He was killed by Criomhthan Niadh Nair and succeeded by him.

Criomhthan son of Lughaidh Riabhdhearg reigned sixteen years. In the twelfth year of his reign (4032 AM) Jesus Christ the God and saviour of the world was born. Criomhtan was very brave and very victorious. He fell from his horse and the fall caused his death. (The reigns of our kings are given in round numbers and seldom are months given.)

In AD 4 Fearadhach Fionn Fachtnach, son of Criomthan, succeeded. His mother was Nar Tath Chaoch, daughter of Laoch, son of Daire who lived in Alba. He was a king of strict justice and moderation. Moran the just judge flourished in his reign. He was the first to wear the Seod Mhorain, which was a collar that, if tied around the neck of a judge who intended to be unjust, would tighten almost to stop his breath, but would instantly enlarge itself as soon as he changed his intention to sincerity. It was used also on witnesses who, if false, would find it contracting so as to throttle them. If a witness was suspect he was warned it would kill him. This king died a natural death at Liathdruim (Leitrim Co. Offaly). He had a reign of twenty years.

In AD 24 Fiathach Fionn then reigned three years. He was the son of Daire Dluthach, Deitsin, Eochaidh, Suin, Roisin, et cetera of Eiremhon's line. From this Fiathach come the Dal bFaitaigh. He fell by Fiachadh Fionnoladh son of Fearaidheach Fionn Feachtnach, Criomhthan Niadh Nair of Eiremhon's line, who reigned twenty-seven years. The non-Gaelic tribes made a feast that they were three years preparing and invited the Gaels who were ruling to come. This went on for nine days till these sprang on the Gaels and slaughtered them. These tribes had three chiefs: Cairbre Cinn Cit, Monarch and Buan. The last two were Firbolg. This took place at Magh Cru (there is a district east of Achad Fhomhair called Aiteachthuaith and this revolt is named from the same word). Fiachadh's wife Eithne, daughter of the king of Alba, Feig's wife Beartha, daughter of the king of Munster, and Aine, daughter of Goirtniad, king of Sacsa escaped to Alba where they gave birth to three sons Tuathal Teachtmhar, Tiobraide Tireach, and Corb Olom. These three queens were spared on account of the advanced state of pregnancy, but they made for Alba for safety.

This event deprived the people of hope and engendered fear and listlessness and soon a famine set in. Many looked for a remedy and the draoi were consulted. Their answer was that the cause of all their misery was the killing of all kings, chiefs and nobles, and that nothing would atone to heaven but a resolve to bring back the heirs from exile and reinstate them. These tribes were pleased with this answer and considered they had suffered enough in twenty-five years of famine and misery and all kinds of calamities so they sent an invitation to the son of Fiachadh Fionnoladh to return to rule Ireland, promising allegiance. They swore by the sun and moon their loyalty, for there was reluctance on the part of the princes to trust them after what happened at Magh Cru. However they had some loyal and reliable Gaels in Ireland and one of these was Fiachaidh Casan who had a cousin Fionbhal and they had gathered five hundred men and greatly troubled the Aitheachthuaith. Tuathal was accompanied by his mother, Eithne who had had him well educated and trained, and his grandfather, the king of Alba, gave him a large force.

In AD 54 Cairbre Cinn Cit took the throne of Ireland after Magh Cru. He was a son of Dubhthaig, Rughraidhe, Diochuin, Tat, Luighre, Oiris, Earnduilbh, Rionoil, son of the king of Denmark, and he had come with Labhradh Loingseach to the fortress of Tuam Teanbhoith, but died of the plague after five years.

Elim then took the throne of Ireland for twenty years. He was son of Conragh, Rughruidhe, Sithrighe, Dubh, Fomhar, Airgeadmhar, Siorlamh, Fionn, Bratha, Labhraidh, Cairbre, son of

Ollamh Fodla of Ir's race. He was slain in the Battle of Aichill (near Tara).

In AD 79 Tuathal Teachtmhar was joined by many who hoped for better things and he headed for Tara and was proclaimed king of Ireland. Elim, as soon as he could, met him at Aichill, was defeated, and slain. Elim's supporters were strongly entrenched in the twenty years and Tuathal had to fight them in twenty-five battles in Leinster, twenty-five in Connacht and twenty-five in Munster.

Soon Ireland began to prosper and despair gave way to joy. As soon as he was able he convened the Feis Teamhrach – where the learned met that goodly laws great Erin get – and he was joyfully accepted and loyalty promised to his house for ever – and to his successors. He enlarged Meath for the Ard-ri taking part from Munster and in it he built the royal palace of Tlachtga, and in it was the sacred fire from which each household had to take its fire at Halloween and pay a scrabble (tri pingne – each pinginn weighing eight grains of wheat) to the king of Munster each year. Sacrifices were offered and consumed by the draoi. He built Uisneach on the part he took from Connacht and here the people came on the first of May and bartered horse, arms, et cetera. The king of Connacht got a horse and arms from each chief, and religious rites were performed. He built Tailtean on the Ulster part, and here the marriages were arranged and the ceremonies performed and an ounce of silver paid by each couple to the king of Ulster. The Aonach Tailtean was held on La Lughnasadh (1st August) and the games were celebrated for this was customary since the reign of King Lugh Lamhfhada. A fourth stately residence he built on the part taken from Leinster on the royal hill of Tara where the Feis Teamhrach was held every third year at which kings, chiefs, judges, draoi, generals, bards and historians met and made laws, collected notable information, verified it, and entered it into the royal records, called the Psalter of Tara – Saltair na Teamhrach. At the table the order of dignity was observed and learned men of all the sciences sat at one side and the usher brought in each person and placed him in his rightful place. Tuathal's daughter Dairine married Eochaidh Ainchean but in a year he went to Tuathal and said she was dead and asked for

LA an LUAIN

Fither, her sister, who, when she saw Dairine alive and well collapsed and could not be revived. Dairine, suspecting nothing, was so overcome at the death of her sister that she threw herself on the body and fell into convulsions and died there and then. Tuathal found out what had happened. He made it known by letters to his supporters who also were very angry at this outrage and sent warriors to him to punish such treachery. Then he entered Leinster with fire and sword, but the Leinster people made an agreement with Tuathal that they and their descendants would give him and the kings of Tara a two-yearly tribute of six thousand cows, six thousand ounces of silver, six thousand fine mantles, six thousand large hogs, six thousand wethers and six thousand brazen caldrons. This Boraimhe Laighean was divided between Connacht, Oirghiall and Tara. It was paid to forty kings of Tara, but it was not without strife at times as it was so heavy. Many years later Saint Moling obtained from King Fianacta that he would not collect it till Monday, but the saint meant La an Luain – the Monday of the Day of Judgement. Tuathal had a general assembly held at Eomhuin Mhacha and another at Cruachan Chrobhdherg where it was seen to that any tampering with the records during the usurpation were or would be corrected. Sixty men who were masters of trades and professions were appointed to examine, and license those up to a sufficient high standard and refuse to license those not of sufficient standard in their own trade or profession. These examiners were called Iollanuidh. Tuathal was slain after thirty years' reign by Mal.

In AD 109 Mal took the throne, son of Rughruidhe, Cathbhadh, Giallchaidh Fionn, Fionnachadh, Muireadhach son of Fiachadh Fionnamhnaig, Irial Glunmhar, Conall Cearnach, Aimhirgin Iargiunnach, Cas Trillseach, Fachtna, Cana, Gionga, Rughruighe Mor, (a quo Clanna Rughruighe) of Ir's race, and he reigned four years till slain by Feidlimidh Reachtmhar, son of Tuathal who reigned nine years. His mother was Baine, daughter of Scal Balbh, a son of the king of 'Breatain'. He administered and enjoined on the judges' strict justice; an eye for an eye, a leg for a leg, a cow for a cow, so that the person who did the injury had to bear the same injury himself. This Lex Talionis greatly restrained wrongdoing and hasty tempers and promoted good behaviour and security of life, limb and property. He died a natural death and was succeeded by Cathaoir Mor.

In AD 122 Cathaoir Mor reigned three years. He was a son of Feidlimidh Fiorurghlas, Cormoc Gealta Gaoth, Nia Corb, Cu Corb, Mogh Corb, Conchubhar Abhradhruadh, Fionn File, Rossa Ruadh, Feargus Fairge, Nuadha Neacht, Seadna Siothbhach, Lughaidh Loithfhionn, Breasal Breac, Fiachaidh Forbric, Oilill Glas, Fearadhach Foghlas, Nuadha Fullon, Ealloit, Art, Mogh Airt, Criomhthan Coscrach, Feidlimidh Foirtruin, Feargus Fortamhail, Breasal Breodhaman, Aongus Ollamh, Oilill Bracain and Labhraidh Loingseach (of Eiremhon's line). He had thirty sons, but twenty died childless. From his son Rossa Failgeach descend O'Connor Failge, O'Diomsaigh, O'Duinn and Clan Colgan. From another son Fiachaidh Aiceadha sprang O'Broin and O'Tuathal, and through Fiachaidh's son Breasal Bealach come Mac Murchadha. Cathaoir fell by Conn in the Battle of Magh Agha (Upper Kells, Co. Meath).

Conn Cead-Cathach son of Feidlimidh Reachtmhar reigned twenty years. Ughna (Una) daughter of the king of Lochloinn was his mother. He fought a hundred battles in Munster, and he gained sixty victories in Ulster and Leinster, and was forced to divide Ireland and to cede to Mogh Nuaghat the southern half which from then was called Leath Mogha, and north of the Eiscir Riada, Leath Cuinn. Mogh won over Conn ten battles namely Brosnach, Samhpait, Sliabh Musach, Gabhran, Suama, Grian, Ath Luain, Magh Croich, where fell Fiachadh Rioghfhada son of Feidlimidh Reachtmhar, Asal, and the Battle of Uisneach. After these came the division.

Tiobraide Tireach's mother had escaped at Magh Cru, but he sent from Ulster to Tara fifty men whom he disguised as women and they murdered Conn when his guard was absent. Conn had treacherously slain Mogh Nuaghat in his bed in the morning of the day they intended to fight the Battle of Maighe Leane. Mogh Nuaghat is known by four names: Eoghan Mor, Eoghan Fidhfheartach and Eoghan Taithlioch. His father was Mogh Neid, son of Dearg, son of Deirgthine of the Heber Finn line, and he had a son, Oilill Olum, and two daughters, Scoithniamh and Coinioll, and their mother was Beara daughter of Eibhear Mor, son of Miodhna, king of Castile in Spain.

Mogh was told by a draoi that after seven years there would be a terrible famine and that he should build storehouses and live mostly on fish and fowl and save and purchase grain. This he religiously did, and when the famine came he fed the country but on condition that they should pay him and the ruler of Munster a constant tribute. This was joyfully complied with and he was highly respected for his piety in respecting the prophesy of the draoi and acting on it efficiently, and the event confirmed that he had done well.

In AD 145 Conaire son of Mogh Lamha, Lughaidh Allathach, Cairbre Cromcinn, Daire Dornmor, Cairbre Fionnmor, Conaire Mor, son of Eidersgoil of Eiremhon's line reigned seven years. His mother was Eithne daughter of Lughaidh Mac Daire. From Conaire descend the Dal Riada of Alba and of Uladh, the Baiscnigh and the Muscruidhe.

He was slain by Neimhidh son of Sraibhghinn, and succeeded by Art, son of Conn Ceadcathach (of the hundred battles) of Eiremhon's line, who reigned thirty years. His wife was Queen Meidhbh Leathdearg daughter of Conann Cualann. From her is named Rath Meidhbhe at Tara. He had three sisters, Maoin, Sadhbh and Saruit, and two brothers, Conla and Crionna, who were killed by Conn's two brothers, Eochaidh Fionn and Fiachadh Suidhe. The sisters are described as beautiful and virtuous. Saruit married Conaire son of Mogh Lamha, and their sons were Cairbre Rioghfhada of the Dalriads of Alba and Ulster; Cairbre Baischaoin and Cairbre Musc. That the same name was given to children of the same family can be accounted for by a prophesy of a draoi that was accepted as true but vague as to whom it might refer. Rioghfhada went to Alba; one of his descendants Eochaidh Muinreamhar (thick neck) had a son called Earc from whom came the Dal Riada of Alba, and a son Olchu from whom came the Dal Riada of Ulster. The Dal Riadhs in Ulster were called An Ruta. Sadhbh married MacNiadh son of Lughaidh of Ith's line, and their son was Lughaidh 'Mac' Con. When MacNiadh died she married Oilill Olum and they had nine sons, but seven were slain at the Battle of Magh Mucruimhe. Their names were Eoghan, Dubhmearchon, Mogh Corb,

Lughaidh, Eochaidh, Diochorb and Tadhg. The others were Cormac Cas and Cian. This Eoghan was slain by Beinne Briot, son of a king in Britain; he was also called Eoghan Mor. He had a son, Fiachadh Fear Da Liach (of two sad events), who was born after his father's death, and his mother died after he was born having delayed his birth for twenty-four hours because her father, who was a draoi, told her that if she could delay the birth that length of time her son would be a king, otherwise he would be a draoi. She was a daughter of Dil, son of Da Chreaga, and her name was Moncha.

From this Fiachadh descend the Clan Carrthaigh, the Clan of Suilleabhain, and their branching septs. From Cormac Cas come the Dal gCais, O'Brians, Mac Mahons, MacNamaras (Siol Aodha), et cetera. In Oilill Olum's first will he left the government of Munster to Cormac Cas but when he heard of Fiachadh's arrival he changed the will, leaving Munster to Cormac for life and then to Fiachadh for life; then it was to alternate between the houses of these two. For many years this will was held in veneration and was dutifully and religiously respected and it brought the blessings of peace and unity, and it maintained friendship and harmony. From Olum's third son Cian came O'Carrol of Ely, O'Meachair, O'Hara, O'Gara and O'Connor Ciannachta, (some came to Dungiven, Co. Derry). Oilill Olum was at first called Aongus but he acquired three blemishes by not respecting three prohibitions a draoi gave him in the use of his spear, and these were occasioned by his doing violence to Aine daughter of Ogamuill who bit off his ear.

Cormac Cas was rated fifth best champion in Ireland in his time, the others were Lughaidh Lamha, Fionn Mac Cumhall, Lughaidh 'Mac' Con, and Cairbre Gailin. No one else was thought fit to fight any of these. This Lughaidh was known as Mac Con to historians because when rather young he was a bit crabbéd and hard to satisfy but they got him a hound and it had the desired effect on him and he became very fond of it and it became his constant companion. It was called Ealoir Dhearg and belonged to Olum who reared and educated him being his stepfather but later in life he banished him when he found that he had given a wrong judgement. He remained in exile for some time, but being of a military disposition he set his aim at the kingship and persuaded Beinne Briot to help him. He did, and so he landed a large force and challenged Art son of Conn (of one hundred battles). Art was slain in a plain near Athenry called Mucraimhe, and Lughaidh followed the defeated army without mercy and inside a week became king.

In AD 182 Lughaidh son of MacNiadh, Luigheach, Daire, Firuillne (fear Uillne), Eadbhuilg, Daire, Siothbhuilg, Fear Uillne, Deaghamhrach, Deagha Dearg, Deirgtheine, Nuaghatt, Airgtheach, Luchtaire, Logha Feidlioch, Eiremhon, Eadaman, Gosamhuin, Sin, Maithsin, Logha, Eadaman, Mal, Lughaidh, son of Ith, son of Breogain became Ard-ri and reigned thirty years. From him came O'Leary, O'Baire of Aronn in Carbry, Magh Flanchy of Dartruidhe, and from his son Fathadh Canann came O'Cuirnin and Mac Aillin of Alba. Lughaidh was the third Ard-ri of Ith's line (the others were Eochaidh Eadgothach, for four years, and Eochaidh Apthach, for one year).

He extended his power greatly over Gall and Alba. He was of the same lineage as the Brigantes who were descended from the eight sons of Breogan, namely Breagha, Fuad, Muirtheimhne, Cuailgne, Eibhle, Bladh, Cuala and Nar.

They were afterwards known to the Irish as Gael-Briot (the name survives in the surname Galbreath). These were the Gaelic inhabitants of Britain. They were first fixed up in Cumberland (cumar – rough ground here) but they spread into most of York, Lancaster, Durham, Westmorland and part of Northumberland. They had asked King Eiremhon to fix them up in Cumberland, and the Picts were friendly neighbours who had gone from Ireland a short time before that. The Ard-ri had helped them to settle in Alba having been refused territory in Leinster a short time after they had arrived from Pictavium (Poitiers), having fled from Thrace under Gud who saved his daughter's virtue by killing Polycorn, king of Thrace. The king in France was kind to them but Gud learned after some time that he also was interested in her, so he and his people (three hundred men) slipped away, taking the French boats and landed in Wexford, but she sickened on the sea and died. Eiremhon fitted them up with the widows of the fallen De Danans and three Gaelic widows. Wars and invasions are very efficient at making widows.

Feircheas, son of Coman Eigeas, at the command of Cormac Mac Airt, slew King Lughaidh (Mac Con) as he stood with his back to a pillar stone distributing gold and silver to bards and learned teachers in the Plain of Gort and Oir (field of gold), Co. Tipperary. He died there and then.

The spear's name was Ringcne. Lughaidh was on his way back from Munster where he had gone to seek help but was not considered worthy of their help because of those of them he had slain at Magh Mucruimhe.

In AD 212 Feargus Dubhdéadach (dubh = black, déad = tooth) succeeded. He had two big black teeth. He was son of Fionchada, Eogamhuin, Fiathach Finn, Daire Dluthach, Deitsin, Eochaidh, Sin, Roisin, Trein, Rothrein, Airiondil, Maine, Forga, Fearadhach, Oiliollaran, Fiach Fear Mara, Aongus Tuirmheach of the line of Eiremhon, but he only ruled one year. Cormac had been banished to Connacht by Feargus and his two brothers after they had taken hostages from him and after Cormac had feasted them in the north of Magh Breagh, at which feast one of their attendants held a torch to Cormac's hair and scorched him severely. Cormac asked Tadhg son of Cian for help. He was powerful in Eile. 'Yes,' said Tadhg, 'if you give me territory.'

'I'll give you as much of Magh Breagh as you will be able to drive your chariot round on the day you beat the three Ferguses.'

'Then,' said Tadhg, 'my grandfather's brother Lughaidh Lamha is in Aherlow beside Sliabh Gcrot (Galteemor); if you bring him he will probably slay the three Ferguses.' Cormac went for him and found him lying in his fianbhoth (hunting booth). Cormac gave him a slight prod with his javelin.

'Who wounds me?'

'Cormac mac Airt.'

'It is well thou didst wound me for I killed your father.'

'Give me an eric for him.' An eric is a fine agreed by the aggrieved party to compensate for a crime or murder committed.

'A king's head in battle,' said Lughaidh.

'Then give me the head of Feargus, king of Ulster, who has come between me and the kingship of Erin.' Feargus had slain Tadhg's father in the Battle of Samhna. This interview had the desired effect. The Battle of Crionna was fought. Tadhg kept Cormac out of the battle on a hill in the rear with an attendant named Deilionn Druit. Cormac changed clothes with him for he knew that Lughaidh was dangerous when his battle fury was on him. Lughaidh came out of the battle with the head of Fergus Foltleabhair (long haired). 'Is that the head of Feargus Dubhdéadach?'

'No, it is his brother's,' said the attendant. He returned again with the head of Feargus Caisfhiaclach, asked the same question and got the same answer.

He returned a third time, put the same question to him and he answered, 'Yes it is.' Lughaidh threw the head at him with such force on the chest that he died on the spot. Then Lughaidh fainted from wounds and loss of blood. This was at Crionna (on Boyne near Stackallen bridge). Tadhg defeated the Ulster army seven times that day and then mounted his chariot and told his driver to include Tara. When they came near Ath Cliath (Dublin), Tadhg who just came out of a faint from three wounds, asked if they had included Tara. 'We have not,' and with that he struck the driver dead. Cormac got his physician to irritate the wounds on the inside while healing them on the outside. He was a year in pain till Lughaidh Lamha went and brought a Munster doctor-surgeon, who at once rectified things. He had heard his groans as he came near with his three pupils, and Tadhg got well in a short time. The surgeon's name was Fingin who was a fear-glic (skilled), whom the bards honoured with an Amhra (poem of praise). Tadhg at once got from Cormac lands in Leinster which he had promised him.

Cormac's mother was Eachtach, daughter of Ulcheatach, a maker of arms, and she had a dream on the night before the Battle of Magh Mucruimhe. Art interpreted it so accurately like history that we who know its literal fulfilment can call it a prehistory or a history of the events before they took place. Cormac's wife was Eithne Ollamhdha, foster daughter of a great and generous man who kept a pot boiling to entertain all who passed by, not asking who they were. Some of the gentry took advantage of his hospitality, staying with him with their families and managed to take away as many cattle and horses as they pleased and this reduced his stock till he had only seven cows and a bull, so he left Dun Buiciodh taking his wife and foster child, Eithne the daughter of Dunluing, with him and went privately to a wood near Kells and built a booth of sods and sticks. Cormac one day saw Eithne and watched her from a distance at her work. He admired the wisdom and the diligence and the carefulness she used at her work and also her beauty and modesty and the cheerfulness and efficiency of this country girl. She was somewhat abashed when a great man rode up to her, saluted her in a reassuring voice, and soon asked for her hand, but she answered him that she would not consent to marry the greatest monarch in the world without the consent of her foster father. 'Who is he? Take me to him.' When he heard he said, 'Why then, your name must be Eithne, the daughter of Dunling.' Buiciodh was pleased at the good fortune of this dear foster child, and Cormac told him he would richly reward him and he gave him the land of Tuath Odhrain (Orantown, Co. Meath).

In AD 213 Cormac Mac Art of Eiremhon's line succeeded after the death of Fergus and reigned for forty years. He had ten beautiful daughters and three sons, Daire, Ceallach and Cairbre. He governed well and wrote a tract for Cairbre called 'Advice to kings' which gives excellent principles for governing. He repaired, enlarged and decorated the Teach Miodcuarta, made it three hundred cubits long, fifty broad and thirty high. A large lanthorn of curious design hung in the centre of this 'house of the going round of mead'. There were fourteen doors connecting with the house, the lodging apartments had a hundred and fifty beds besides the king's bed, and a hundred and fifty champions who also served at table when he dined in public. The house guards consisted of, among others, a thousand and fifty of his best and bravest soldiers. He was most generous and liberal and free, so lavish, in fact, that he invaded Munster to obtain tribute, and used Irish and Albian (Scottish) draoi against the Munster army under Fiacha Muilleathan, who in great straits sent to Kerry for Modharuth, who would only consent to come and deliver the Munster army if he was given and confirmed in two territories. These two territories were later named Roches and Condons after the Norman invasion. This was granted and he delivered them.

They were so enraged at the miseries they had been subjected to by Cormac's draoi that they asked Fiacha to lead them against him. He led them and Cormac and his men fled and were pursued and forced to give Fiacha hostages and compensation for any loss inflicted on Munster.

Cormac exacted the Boru Laighean. He fought thirty-six battles. He had a mill erected at Tara for grinding meal, having sent to Scotland for an engineer. He made it a law that every monarch should have a lord, a judge, a draoi, a doctor, a poet, a historian, a musician and three stewards. Cormac lost an eye defending his son Ceallach, who had put out the eyes of a person who had committed some misdemeanour and whom Cormac would not pardon, but did so at last when Aongus Gaothbhuailteach, who was very expert in military matters, gave bail for his future good conduct. Aongus was a son of Fiachadh Suidhe, son of Conn (of one hundred battles). He slew Ceallach for doing this to a pardoned person who was also his friend. The principal men considered it bad luck to have a king with a blemish reside at Tara, so Cormac took up residence at Machuill, not far away, and lived privately and wrote a copy of the Psalter of Tara and supervised a work on Laws and on Obedience due to Princes written by Fiatach, also the Teagasc Riogh for his son Cairbre. In it, as in a dialogue, he considers a king's duty as legislator, as soldier, as statesman and as scholar. He also treats of the laws of poets, philosophers, draoi and antiquarians.

Seven years before his death he received the Light of the Gospel. Maoilegan the draoi demanded that he conform to the religion of his ancestors but he gave him the answer that it was beneath the dignity of a human to adore a brute (golden calf) but the draoi did not take that answer as final, so he took it away and came back with it lavishly decorated.

'Won't you now adore a deity of such splendid majesty?' Cormac told him that he would only adore the supreme God, the Creator of the heavens and the earth and of a place of punishment for the wicked who corrupt His worship and disobey his laws. That same evening a bone of a fish at supper choked him and it was said that this was brought about by Maoilegan and infernal fiends, but before he died he gave orders not to bury him in the royal sepulchre of Brugh Os Boinn (Newgrange). His command was not obeyed but as they were carrying the body across the Boyne at Ath Fuaid (ford of the Bier) the river suddenly rose and overflowed and at their fourth attempt it swept the body away from them into the water and threw it on shore at Rosnariogh where it was buried. (Saint Colmcille who was born in AD 521 found Cormac's head and reburied it and said thirty Masses for him, and a church was later built there.)

Finn Mac Cool asked Cormac for his daughter Grainne, but she did not want him and had watched one of Finn's men, a young man called Diarmuid O'Duibhne, who was the star at a game of hurley the same day at which Cormac's team were beaten on the Plain of Tara by Finn's team. When Cormac saw he was beaten he got them to play in the other direction, so they did, but Diarmuid still saw to it that the Fianna won. At the supper she showed preference for him and put him under geis (an honour bond that it was disgraceful not to fulfil) to elope with her. In this great dilemma he consulted Ossian Finn's son, but he agreed that he was in honour bound by the geis (gaesh). She saw to the arrangements. After a fruitless chase Finn got Grainne's sister Eilbhe from Cormac. Finn's men who took part in the chase were not as anxious as Finn to capture them, and once they had him surrounded, but with his two spears and a race he pole-jumped over a line of them and got lost.

Finn was leader of the Leinster Fianna whose duties were to defend Ireland, to support the king with arms, to ferret out pirates lurking in creeks and to secure the honour, liberty, life and property of the people of Ireland. They were high-principled men, obedient to their officers and to the laws of Finn. A recruit needed to be able to compose poetry and have a good knowledge of the twelve books of poetry, to be master of his arms and of his shield, able to defend himself in flight, excelling in running and jumping, active, agile and able to hold his weapon steady, able to leap perfectly over what was as high as his forehead. He had to be charitable and relieve the poor. If he wanted to marry he was to choose a wife without regard to her means but for her virtue, courtesy and good manners and not follow the custom of insisting on a dowry. He was obliged to never offer violence to a woman.

In the Brehon Law, rape was punishable by death without the possibility of reprieve, even by the High king, so well were women protected and their honour safe-guarded.

In AD 253 Eochaidh Gunnad son of Fiachi, Iomachaidh, Breasal, Fionchada, Fiachadh Fionn, Dluthaig, Deitsin and Sin of the race of Eiremhon was elected but only reigned one year till slain by Lughaidh Feirtre.

Cairbre Liffeachair, having come of age, succeeded his father Cormac (he was twenty-five) who was alive, but blemished. He reigned twenty-seven years till he lost his life in the Battle of Gabhra, wounded by Oscar, grandson of Finn, but slain by Simeon son of Ceirb (from Cork). The fraternal slaughter of Gabhra was dreadful. A dozen of Finn's men survived. The nobility of Ireland perished.

Cairbre was determined, even at the cost of his own life, to wipe out Finn's men, and though they were very brave, a dispute before the battle reduced their numbers so much that they were hopelessly outnumbered by the forces of Cairbre, whose troops even before this were much more numerous. Ossian who was long-lived, answered Saint Patrick's question if he reached Oscar his son while he was still able to speak, 'I stood over my son at the close of the slaughter, Caoilte stood over his six sons, the survivors of the Fianna stood over their dead relatives. It was a scene never to be forgotten. Oscar was found lying on his left elbow, his shield beside him, his lance in his right hand, his blood flowing over his tunic. Ossian his father dropped his spear and uttered a wail, thinking of his own fate when Oscar was gone. He looked into his father's face in utter hopelessness and extended his two hands in a fruitless effort to rise. Ossian took his son's hand and sat on the ground beside him on his left and Oscar had just strength enough to say, 'The Gods be eternally praised, Father, that you are alive and well.'

'Caoilte came and found Oscar's entrails shattered with his backbone and traced how far Cairbre's lance had penetrated, and his arm was buried to the elbow. Caoilte tried with words to revive him but it was useless. He fell down, wringing his hands, hair and beard. That night they kept vigil over Oscar and the slaughtered. Noble Oscar they bore on their spear-shafts to a clear mound and examined him from head to foot; except on the face there was not a hand's breadth free of wounds.' (Oscar was buried on the northern side of Gabhra in a grave and Ossian who was a poet concluded by praying to the king of the world and Patrick that his voice may grow weak as his grief that night was overwhelming.)

Ossian, in his old age, was taken into the Familia of Saint Patrick and looked after, but often drew a rather disparaging comparison between Patrick's table and the lavish spread of the Fianna. Patrick so enjoyed listening to his tales that he became uneasy, thinking he was wasting too much of his missionary time listening to him. An angel appeared to him and said, 'You are not wasting time listening to these, take them down, they will be of value to posterity.'

In AD 281 Fathach Airgtheach and Fathach Cairptheach, brothers, reigned jointly for almost one year. They were sons of Lughaidh Mac Con of Ith's line. Cairptheach was slain by his brother but he himself was soon dethroned and killed by the Fianna Eireann in the Battle of Ollarbha (ol a rú a), near Larne.

Fiachadh Sreibhthuine son of Cairbre succeeded and ruled thirty years. He was married to Aoife, daughter of the king of Gallgaedheal (Galloway). Their son Muireadhach Tireach led an army into Munster and was victorious, but his cousins, the sons of Eochaidh Duibhlan feared he might banish or kill them for something they had done, made war of ambition on their uncle and he was slain in the Battle of Dubhchomair – so called from a draoi who foretold him that if he was killed his posterity would rule, but if the three Collas were slain, theirs would rule. He accepted death for the honour and benefit of his posterity, and Colla Uais was proclaimed king, son of Eochaidh Duibhlan, son of Cairbre Liffeachair (Eiremhon's line) and he was just able to reign for four years till he was driven out of the kingdom. The three brothers fled to Alba to the king, their grandfather for their mother Oileach was his daughter. After three years in Alba they wanted to come home and to have themselves killed to fulfil the prophesy, so that their posterity would reign. They had been well liked in Alba and the king had entered three hundred of their followers into his army pay. The three set out for Tara, each took

COLLA UAIS

only nine men and they were admitted to the king's presence, Muireadhach Tireach who, to their surprise and wonderment, received them as friends and asked them what news they had from Alba, and if they were dejected at the state of their fortune. They told him how surprised they were at the friendship of the person whose royal father they had slain and that his killing pained them to think about. The king answered that clemency was one of the brightest jewels in the crown of princes and therefore he was contented to forgive them and leave them to the judgement and justice of the gods and to the sharp remorse of their conscience, which was the most severe torment of the guilty. In proof of his friendship he settled a princely revenue on them and made them generals in his army. He, after some years, reasoned with them that their salaries would cease at death and that they should provide for their children. He recommended Ulster to them for the insult they had done to Cormac their great grandfather in burning his beard and banishing him to Connacht, and he offered them considerable help in the invasion. They accepted and were surprised to find that seven thousand Ulster natives joined up with them and also forces they had got from Connacht, for the men of Connacht had taken them into military fosterage when they went there before they invaded Ulster.

The province of Connacht marched with them with seven battalions and these sustained the fight for six days. The Collas fought the seventh battle, in which Feargus Fodha was slain and his men were defeated and pursued with great loss from Carn Eochaidh Leathdhearg in Fearmuighe to Gleanrighe. Then they came to Eomhuin Mhacha, plundered it and burned most of it, and it ceased to be inhabited. (The night after they fought, the land subsided and the underneath water squirted up into the hollow then formed on the surface. This area, now a lough, is the present day Lough Neagh and prior to the formation of this lough the River Bann went through this area. This is now why the river has retained its name, Upper and Lower Bann). Colla Uais took territory west of the Bann and west of the new lough. His name was Cairioll.

Colla Meann (Aodh) about Cremorne, and Colla Da Chrioch (Muireadhach) took Upper and Lower Slane. Muireann the daughter of Fiachaidh, the king of Cinel Eoghain, was the wife of Muireadhach Tireach, and it is from him that the Clanna Neill are descended. He was slain by Caolbhach son of Cronn Badhraoi, Eochaidh, Cobha, Lughaidh, Rossa, Iomchaidh, Feidlimidh, Cas, Fiachadh-Aruidhe, Aongus Gaibion, Feargus-Foghlas, Tiobraide Tireach, Breasal, Fearb, Mal, Rochruidhe, Cathbhadh, Giallchadh, Cunnchaidh, Fionnchaidh, Muireadhach, Fiachadh Fionnamhaus (triplets), Irial Glunmhar and Conal Cearnach (of Ir's line) who succeeded and reigned one year. Inneacht, daughter of Lughaidh, was his mother.

He was slain by Eochaidh Moighmheodhin, son of Muireadhach Tireach (Eiremhon's line) and he ruled seven years. He married Mong Fionn and his four sons were Brian, Fiachradh, Feargus and Oilioll.

Before she died he married Carthan Cas Dubh, daughter of the king of Cambria (England was divided into Cambria and Lagria and Armorica took the name Britain, later Bretagne). Their son was Niall. Eochaidh fought the Battle of Cruachan Claonta against Eanna, king of Leinster, and a draoi was taken as a prisoner. His name was Ceadnathach, and when Eanna came on the scene he asked why they had spared him.

'You would never conquer from this hill if I were to live.' Eanna speared him and, as the spear pierced him, Eanna gave an ugly laugh. 'That is an insulting laugh, and it will be a reproach to all your posterity for it will give them a name that will not be forgotten.' This proved true, and they are known as the Ui Cinn-Seallach (ceann = head, Sallac = foul or dirty). Eanna defeated Eochaidh in this disastrous conflict and is recorded to have won thirteen battles. He put Leath Cuinn under tribute to either pay up or die.

He died in peace at Tara and was succeeded by Criomhthan (Criffin) son of Fiodhuig, Daire Cearb, Oilioll Flanbeg, Fiachadh Muilleathan, Eoghan Mor, Oilioll Olum (Heber Finn's line) and he reigned seventeen years. Fidheang was his wife and she was a daughter of the king of Connacht. He established with force his sway over Alba, Lagria and France and took hostages, making them pay tribute. He gave the kingdom of Munster to Conal Eachluath, son of Lughaidh Lamhdhearg, but this was not in accord with the will arrangement of Oilioll Olum, and when the position was examined and it was decided that he had no legal right to it, he abdicated in favour of the rightful heir, Corc son of Lughaidh, who was senior. It was also agreed that at his death it would go to Conal or to his son, and then to alternate with the line of Cormac Cas. Criomhthan was so impressed by this man's integrity that he trusted him as much as to place him in charge of his Irish and foreign hostages, and he proved worthy and gave help to the Ard-ri. He also entrusted the prisoners to him.

Mongfhionn Criomhthan's sister wanted her son Brian to be king, so at Inis Dornghlas on the Moy she prepared poison for him, but as he was reluctant to take it or drink it she, to encourage him and show him it was good, tasted some of it herself and died. But he also took some and died from it at Sliabh Uidhe an Riogh (lower Bunratty). From her sons Brian and Fiacra came the kings of Connacht, called the Ui Briuin (Brune) and the Ui Fiacrach.

In AD 379 Niall, son of Eochaidh Moighmheodhin and Carthan Cas Dubh, daughter of the king of Britain succeeded, and reigned twenty-seven years. Inne, daughter of Lughaidh and widow of Fiachadh, was his first queen. His second consort was Rioghneach, and they had seven sons: Laoghaire, Eanna, Maine, Eoghan, Cairbre and two called Conal.

Niall's help was asked by the Gaels of Alba, (Scotland) and when his strong force fixed things for them they asked him to change the name of Alba to Scotia. 'All right,' he agreed, 'but it must be Scotia Minor, we must leave Scotia Major for Eire.' Scotia came from the Irish who were called Scoti.

Then, under provocation, he led his large army into Lagria, fixed things to his satisfaction and then in an innumerable fleet he crossed to Armorica, north France or Brittany, then called Briton. England became Great Britain to distinguish it from the Britons who earlier colonised Armorica under a Roman general and drove out the natives. Thus we get in French Grande Bretange for Great Britain and Bretange for northern France. He plundered the country and brought from there two hundred, some as hostages and others as slaves. Among the slaves were the sixteen-year-old boy Patrick and his two sisters, Lupita and Darerca. This was in the ninth year of Niall's reign. Things became so bad for what is now England and Wales that, as Stowe relates at the fifty-second page of his British Chronicle, they invited the Saxons to come to save them. They came under Hingust and Horsa whose aid was successful, but they became so pleased with the climate and the soil fertility, et cetera that they decided to stay and treacherously killed four hundred and eighty of the nobility and gentry at one time. So Aurelius Ambrosius, then the king of the country, caused stones that had been brought by Merlin long before from Mount Claire in Munster to be erected where the murders took place as an eternal monument of their cruelty. Aurelius was afterwards buried there. This monument was first called Chorea Gigantum but later called Stonehenge. The Irish had brought these stones from Africa, and not two of them were brought from the same part of Africa. (Perhaps for the same purpose as lead is used in yachts.)

Niall, having tasted so much success against places held by the Romans, went directly this time to France and raided around the River Loire, where he was joined by the forces of Scotia Minor under Gabhran, son of Domhanguirt (doangort), and they had brought Eochaidh son of Eanna Cinnsalach with him, but Niall would not be reconciled with him. Eochaidh had been banished for he had tried to become Ard-ri, for which purpose he lived at Tara nine nights and nine days, but a draoi solemnly advised him on the impiety of doing such, and he took the wise advice and abandoned Tara. On his way home he called to the house of Laidhgin son of Bairceadha, a principal draoi and friendly to the Ard-ri. The draoi's son said something uncomplimentary to Eochaidh, who killed him on the spot.

The father complained to Niall who made war on Eochaidh but at the advice of Laidhgin stopped hostilities on condition that Eochaidh be handed over to them.

This was done, and an iron belt put round him with a chain attached to be put by nine deputed men through a hole in a high standing stone. He wrenched the chain free and with it killed some and, being a good runner, escaped and made his way to his ruling relatives in Scotia Minor.

Niall had other things against him about tributes. In Scotia Minor Eochaidh's wife Feidlin, daughter of Cobhthain, son of

Dathi, had twin boys, and Gabhran's wife Ingeanach was delivered of a daughter as was usual with her. They were delivered in the same room the same night and only the midwife was allowed to be present. At the urgent request of Ingeanach, who was a very dear friend of Feidlin (Fellin), the wife of Eochaidh gave away one of the twin boys and Gabhran's wife took it into her bed and the doors were opened. Gabhran was overjoyed, kissed and embraced it, and called it Aodhan (Ian). The other was called Brandubh. After Niall was dead, Eochaidh returned and resumed the kingship of Leinster. Brandubh succeeded him and Aodhan (Ian) became king of Scotia Minor by hereditary right. When he had firmly established himself and gathered a strong army and navy he came to Leinster in his ambition to rule in Ireland because he was strong and thought himself descended from Cairbre Riada, (ree-a-da), but his real mother, who lived in Leinster, told him who he was, so he sent to Scotia Minor to have this verified. It was, and secrecy was enjoined and kept and there were no more hostilities. He returned a wiser man, fearing the consequences if it became known.

The southern Ui Neill descend from Niall's sons Maine, Laoghaire, Conal-Creamhthainne, and Fiac. In his absence Maine was Ard-Comhairce Eireann Uile (Regent) and his territory was from Cruachan to Loch Ribh. O'Sionach, Magamhaidhe, Mag Carron, O'Broin, O'Quin, and O'Dalaigh are from him. Laoghaire got from Trim to Tara and the O'Cuindealbhain are from him. Conal-Creamhthuinne (Criffinc) got land in Magh Breagha and the O'Maolseachlainn are from him.

Fiac got land around Uisneach and from him come Mac Geoghagans and O'Molloys. The northern O'Niall (Neill) got Tir Eoghain (Tyrone), left by Niall in his will, and from him are the O'Neills. Conal Gulban got Tir Chonail and the O'Donnels are from him. Cairbre, the eldest, got land about Lough Erne, and Eanna got Tir Eanna in Donegal (cf Drumennan) containing 'the Lagan'.

Niall's nine hostages were from Munster, Leinster, Ulster, Connacht, Picts, Scots of Scotia Minor, Brigantes, Armoric-Britons and from Normandy. Eochaidh shot Niall with an arrow across the Loire. Niall's body was brought back from the bank of the river Loire by his nephew Fearadhach and he had him buried in Roilig na Riogh (Cruachan) with great pomp. He took over the government in AD 405.

In AD 405 Fearadhach, better known as Dathi, meaning the active, son of Fiachradh son of Eochaidh Moighmheodhin of Eiremhon's line reigned for twenty-three years. His first consort was Fial daughter of Eachach, his second was Eithne daughter of Orach, who is the mother of Oilioll Molt, his third was Ruadh daughter of Artigh Uicht-leathan, son of Fear Congha, but she died in travail bringing forth Fiachadh Ealgach.

Fighting against the Roman Empire he penetrated as far as the Alps and when he pillaged a Christian Penitentiary of a hermit called Parmenius, he cursed him and a flash of lightning descended on his crown. They brought the body back and buried it at Roilig na Riogh.

From the times that Tuathal Teachtmhar imposed the punishing tribute on Leinster and the dividing of Ireland between Conn and Eoghan, the foundation of internal peace became more unstable than it had been when the contention was for the Ard-ri-ship which assured the holder of an immortal place in the history of Ireland and was striven for by force of arms by those descended from Golamh Mileadh, a king in Spain whose children led the Gaels to Ireland ten hundred and eighty years after the world was drowned, which happened in the six hundredth year of the life of our ancestor Noah, in the year of the world sixteen hundred and fifty-six.

The O'Connor Faly are from Cathaoir Mor and from his son, Rossa Failge, come the O'Dempseys and the O'Dunns. Cathaoir Mor had thirty sons in total and from his son Fiachadh are the O'Tooles, O'Byrnes, O'Dowling, O'Ryan, O'Muldoon, O'Cormach and O'Duffy.

In AD 427 Laoghaire succeeded Dathi. He was a son of Niall, his mother was Roighneach. In the fourth year of his reign, Pope Celestine commissioned Patrick with proper powers and sent him into Ireland to bring the Gospel Faith to Ireland. He was in his sixty-first year. Seeing the divine hand in the miracles that the Lord did through the Bishop Patrick to enable him to overcome the native religion of the draoi in favour of the religion that

Patrick said his God sent him to take to the Irish, and seeing that the draoi could not overcome so powerful a man, he let him have a free hand in teaching, preaching and establishing the faith. The Irish had had many prophesies of his coming. Laoghaire guaranteed his safety, but did not become a Christian because of a sworn promise he made to his father. Being a well-educated man, intelligent and wise who wanted the good of his subjects, he helped Patrick to Christianise Ireland. So Saint Patrick set about converting the whole island, placing bishops, priests and settling monks and nuns in religious houses with endowments. A mint was set up in Armagh and Cashel, learning was catered for, histories and genealogies preserved, books were multiplied, laws adjusted to Christianity, the Resurrection taught, idolatry abolished, tales of the Fianna Eireann written and mostly versified, the Divine Life lived nourished by an tAifreann (Mass), the bread of life, unity in religion and unity in truth safeguarded, miracles worked and the dead raised to life confirming the Faith of Christ. Laoghaire's son Lughaidh was one of those raised from the dead. As Michael the archangel extracted what choked Lughaidh, the queen, his mother in thanksgiving and veneration on her knees received the boy alive from Saint Patrick who had fasted and prayed for three nights and three days imploring God to restore him to life. Patrick told her how Saint Michael had helped, and she made a vow to never forget this favour and promised to bestow annually one sheep of every flock she had and a part of all the provisions that came to her table during her life upon the poor, and to thank and honour the archangel. To perpetuate the memory of the miracle it was ordained by law that all Christian converts should offer the same oblations. It is known in Irish as Cuid Mhichill (vee-hill) and is now called Lamb Sunday. The raising of the boy took place on the feast of Saint Michael. The queen was baptised before she was married, her name was Aongus, a daughter of the general who commanded the army of the king of the Ui Liathan.

During Saint Patrick's sixty-one years as missionary, three hundred and fifty-five bishops were consecrated and three thousand priests ordained. Armagh, at the instruction of an angel, was chosen as the See of the archbishop and Primate of Ireland.

HISTORIANS

Cashel got an archbishop and he was obedient to the archbishop of Armagh. (Travel problems and waste of time were avoided by having bishops and priests near their work.)

Aongus, king of Cashel, dedicated twelve of his sons and twelve of his daughters to the service of God. By direction of Saint Patrick he kept two bishops, ten priests and seventy-two religious men to attend in court to say Mass and to pray for his own happiness and the happiness of the whole kingdom. Patrick was his spiritual director.

Aongus ordained that the Christians should pay three pence to the church, but because the collecting of this would distract the clergy from other more important work it was decreed to give the church five hundred cows, five hundred sheep, five hundred bars of iron, five hundred shirts, five hundred mantles, and that the tax (one scraball = three old pence) be paid to the king in lieu of this. This was observed yearly to the time of Cormac mac Cuillinan. Saint Patrick, when asked, declined to do an examination of the ancient records and genealogies but asked Leary (Laoghaire) to summon to one place the principal clergy, historians and antiquarians for this purpose. These selected nine of their best; Saint Patrick, the pious Benen, the judicious Cairneach, Leary, Daire king of Ulster, Cork king of Munster, Dubhthach mac Ui Lughair, Fithall Feargus, and Rosa mac Tirchin 'nicely versed in foreign tongues'.

Their work was exact and is known as 'The Great Antiquity' and was never disputed. The king, with the consent of his nobles, ordained that these records be committed to the trust and keeping of the reverend prelates of Ireland. These had them transcribed and laid up in their principal churches for use of scholars and for the benefit of posterity to give the Gaels their historical anchorage, and to settle with justice and learning claims based or genealogy and family rights.

It was a law from of old that an erring historian was degraded as was also a judge if he erred through ignorance or bribes of favourites. Just laws fence peace, just administration fortifies it.

King Leary summoned a great convention at Tara. Hereat the laws and records were read. Leary at this parliament resided in the Teach-miodcuarta, the king of Ulster in the house called Eachruis

THE FLOOD

Uladh, the king of Connacht in Coisir Chonnachtach, the king of Munster in Lung Muimhneach and the king of Leinster in the house called Lung Laighneach. Lung signified a house and is used for a big boat or ship. Those who came to Ireland in boats lived in them as in houses for some time, and of course Noah, our ancestor, lived in the Ark that served as boat and house. The business took place in the Teach-miodcuarta, the queens had a house to themselves with separate apartments, it was called Grianan na nIngean.

The king sat with his back to the east, the king of Munster on his left, the king of Ulster on right, the king of Leinster facing him, and the king of Connacht behind him.

Three other houses on Tara were Carcar na nGiall (na neal) (for hostages and state prisoners). Realta na bhFileadh, where the poets, judges and the antiquarians transacted their business, and the other was the Grianan na nIngean; the women's quarters.

Leary gave external submission to the true religion, and Patrick got on well with him intellectually, politically and religiously and in safety but Patrick did not approve of his not believing and told him that none of his descendants would be king, but the queen besought him not to curse her unborn child, so he said he would not curse Lughaidh till he opposed him. Patrick added: 'Because you have believed in God and done my will long life will be given to you, but neither king nor crown prince save Lughaidh and I will not curse him till he opposes me'.

When he did he was killed by lightning.

Leary had many admirable qualities which appeared during his reign and in the transition from the religion of the draoi to the true religion.

We give here the names of some of the outstanding authors who wrote the events in Ireland in the time of the draoi: Aimhergin Glungeal, Sean Macaighe, Brigh Banaghdar (a quo the word brigh), Conla Caoin Bhreathach, Seanchan Mac Cuil Chlaoin, and his learned son Fachtna, Seanchan son of Oiliolla, Moran son of Maoin, Feargus Fianaidhe in Kerry-Luachra, Feircheairtine a poet, Neidhe son of Aidhna (i-na), Aitherne, Feargus a poet son of Aitherne, Neara son of Fionchuil from Siodubh, Seadamus son of Moruinn, Fearadach Fionnfathach, the chief author of the wisdom of the king of Ireland, Fithall Feargus, a poet, Rosa and Dubhthach, the three who delivered the annals and public records to Saint Patrick. (When Sean Macaighe delivered an unjust sentence many large blisters broke out visibly on his right cheek.)

Leary was taken prisoner by Criomhthan king of Leinster at Ath Dara, where his forces were slaughtered. Criomthan would only release him if he swore to never again lay claim to the Boru Laighean or exact that tribute. He swore, but broke his oath and was killed by lightning at Greallagh Doyle on the fruitful Liffey Plain. He has left posterity an example and a salutary lesson that oaths should not be trifled with.

In AD 453 Oilioll Molt succeeded and reigned twenty years. He was a son of Dathi whose wife was Uchtdealbh, daughter of Aongus son of Nadfraoch. The lady Fial visited her before the baby was born and the mother got a great longing for a bit of mutton (molt) so the lady insisted on the names. In his reign a coarbha of Saint Patrick died (a priest of a religious order ordained by Saint Patrick). Oilioll was defeated and slain in the Battle of Ocha by Lughaidh, son of Leary aided by Mortoch mac Earca (mother) son of Eoghan, Feargus Cearbheoil, Conall Creamhtuine and Fiachadh Lonn son of Caolbhadh king of Dalraidhe. Before this Oilioll Molt had had a Pyrrhic victory fighting against the people of Leinster at Tuam-Aicher. The slaughter on both sides was very great.

In AD 473 Lughaidh, son of Leary, whom Saint Patrick raised, succeeded and reigned twenty years. In the tenth year of his reign Pope Felix the Third was elected.

In the nineteenth year of his reign his great benefactor Saint Patrick died on Wednesday, 17th March, AD 493 aged over one hundred and twenty years after sixty-one years of very active missionary work. In twenty-one years he had gone around Ireland. He had established bishops, priests and religious all over the kingdom and they were doing the work well in the grace and love of the Lord Jesus. And Patrick revisited the churches and cloisters, et cetera and supervised things.

He had the Brehon code of laws made to harmonise with the teaching of the Lord Jesus. He fixed appropriate revenues for the

See of Armagh for it was by the command of God's angel that he chose Armagh as his residence and See. Here we quote from the Book of the Angels:

> Moreover it (the See of Armagh) is to be venerated on account of that priceless treasure which it possess by a secret arrangement; namely the most precious blood of Jesus Christ in the linen winding sheet, together with the relics of other saints preserved in the southern church where repose the bodies of the holy pilgrims from afar beyond the sea together with relics of Patrick and the other holy men, Peter, Paul, Stephen and Laurance.

Patrick wanted to die in Armagh:

> 'I choose the place where I shall rise
> 'And open eyes on Resurrection Day.
> 'Armagh my love, Armagh my dove.
> 'Armagh above the saints I sway.
> 'But choice I have not got in this,
> 'I seek my bliss in will of God.
> 'But haunt it will my soul
> 'That hill, I'll love it still 'neath other sod.'
> 'It will be waste where Macha built,
> 'Where heroes dwelt and glory shed,'
> Said angel. 'No, Your sway shall go o'er it
> 'And flow o'er quick and dead.'

Before Patrick came to Ireland he went to an island in the Tyrrhene Sea and found a new house in which a holy person called Justus dwelt with his wife, and both looked young. He enquired who were the old and decrepit people with them and was told: 'These are our descendants. When the Lord Jesus came here on earth he came here as a visitor, and as it was our custom to be hospitable to visitors and to strangers we entertained him, not knowing who he was, but before he left he said to us, 'I am Jesus Christ whose members you have been ministering to even as now you have done to myself.' Then he gave us a walking stick and told us to keep it for a man called Patrick who would visit us in later times. Then, after he had blessed us and our house, and gave us the gift of keeping young (but we did not have power to transmit that to our children), He went up to heaven. 'It is for you.' But Patrick said, 'No, I will not take it unless I get it from the Lord himself and so confirm the gift as from himself.' He stayed about three days. Later on he was on Mount Morion near Capua and the Lord appeared to him and commanded him to preach the Gospel to the Irish People and at the same time gave him the staff, which is called Bachall Iosa, or the staff of Jesus, to be his stay in weakness and his defence in adversity; and many wonders were wrought by its use. Saint Bernard lets us know that it was gold-covered and adorned with most precious gems. (The town of Ballyboughal gets its name from it.)

One day in Patrick's old age he was preaching at Saul and Saint Brigid and several of her nuns were present. A luminous cloud came down from the sky and stood awhile in mid-air and close to the assembly. Then it moved slowly and settled over Dun Da Leith Glas (now Downpatrick).

Full of awe and afraid to ask Patrick they asked Brigid who, at the bidding of Patrick, explained the vision thus: 'Patrick's angel is borne in that cloud of glory, he has come here first to show us that Patrick will die here and his body remain here some days, and then the angel went to the fort of Down to show that Patrick's body will be taken from here to be buried in Down Patrick, and there it will remain till the Day of Judgement. I too and another saint (Colmcille) shall rest in the same grave and we shall rise together from that tomb on the Last Day.'

All the people were amazed and praised God, and Patrick asked Brigid to weave with her own hands his winding sheet. She promised and had it ready and brought it to Saul when he died.

As Patrick had been setting out from Saul to go to Armagh, God's angel said to him, 'Return to Saul. There you shall die, but your petitions have been granted by God, that is to say, first, that Armagh shall be the seat of your jurisdiction, second that whoever on the day of his death shall recite the hymn composed in your honour will have you with the right to fix the penalty for his sins. Third, that the children of Dichu who received you with so much kindness shall obtain mercy and not perish for ever, fourth, that all the Irish in the Day of Judgement shall be judged by you, that is all those whose apostle you have been, even as the Lord said to the twelve apostles, 'You shall sit on twelve thrones judging the twelve tribes of Israel.'

The angel said to Patrick, 'Let two wild oxen be chosen, let them go wherever they will. Where they shall stop a church shall be built in honour of thy poor body. And lest the relics of thy body be taken from the grave let a cubit of earth rest over thy body.' (That is, a man's cubit which is what a man standing can reach with his arm – about seven or eight feet.) The oxen were brought from Clogher.

Patrick received the Body of Christ from Bishop Tassach according to the angel Victor's counsel and then sent his holy soul to heaven. His body was kept twelve days in the church of Saul. Deepest grief came over Ireland, there was no night darkness in Magh Inis for an angelic radiance lit up the plain. Ireland's elders heard the singing of angelic choirs and a great host of heaven's angles came to wake the body on the first night (Wednesday, 17th March, AD 493) and they kept watch themselves and chanted the usual psalms (the human watchers had fallen asleep). When the angels were going away they left a sweet fragrance of honey and wine. On the other nights the men kept watch, praying and singing psalms.

The Amhra or poem of praise of Saint Patrick was written by Saint Seachnall in Latin but here put into an Ancient Irish metre for those who speak English.

> O hear all you who love the Lord
> These deeds accord with angel acts
> That Patrick did nor are they hid
> We lift but lid off known facts
>
> In life he did the will of God
> In Erin trod the hard hard way
> His works still shine with light divine
> The faith that's mine has come to stay

That faith he held in firm grasp
And he did clasp our Isle there to
Our church he built, ... our saints have knelt
His presence felt some got a view

The Lord himself had chosen him
When light was dim in our green isle
To net us in keep us from sin
Put on our chin a holy smile

He sowed in Erin the faith of Christ
Soon fruit was twice what he did sow
It was good seed there grew no weed
The soil with speed increase did show

With joy God's faithful messenger
The lesson here gives forth to all
With word and fact with truth and act
With strong contact did idols fall

He lives in Christ's eternal joy
He served as boy he served as man
As angel of God up and down he trod
The Irish sod once he began

He gloried in the cross of Christ
For him sufficed if God was pleased
He had his share of cross to bear
Nor did he care when cold him freezed

He feeds to converts bread of life
Lest in hell's strife they might be weak
He gives them priests to give God's feasts
As flock increased then they more seek

Angelic virtue he showed and taught
As good priest ought and Church requires
As temple host of Holy Ghost
As virtue most that God desires

The Gospel light that Patrick lit
All can see it as set on high
The Lord has owned it none have dethroned it
Say not He loaned it 'twas gift for aye

Great in heaven will he be called
Who has not stalled in word nor deed
He kept concord with word of Lord
Brought law and order and reign of Creed

To Gaels the Gospel tale he tells
Amongst them dwells and brings salvation
He brings God's Grace to every face
Has Mass replace false adoration

Nor treats he different soul of slave
From warrior brave or royal king
He sought earth's great to advance the state
Of church that lately he did bring

Lest any one of converts fall
He prays for all at holy Mass
He suffers well lest even smell
Of sin and hell o'er them trespass

The flock was good the pastor better
Both by letter (Epistle) and Gospel fed
By faith defined and law combined
He us entwined to Rome who led

This Pontiff great the Lord had sent
and him He meant to rule and lead
His household great the Irish state
By clerics' weight convert with speed

This messenger of Heaven's king
To us did bring the invitation
To Heaven's feast the great the least
Layfolk and priest of sinless nation

In studying the Sacred Book
He took a look at God made man
Took Israel's place by life of grace
And left his race and native land

Faithful son of Catholic Church
Not left in lurch by error's night
She still keeps true the old the new
And not a few errors does fight

Great cultivator of the field
That it may yield fruit Christ has sown
He sowed no fears in pious ears
Repentant tears towards grace have grown

As vicar of Christ who slaves redeems
He frees in streams poor captives chained
By lack of light by hopeless night
At such a sight this priest was pained

For monks and nuns God's cloisters great
He was not late to have erected
To chant God's praise in hymnal lays
To spread faith's rays have souls perfected

> In prayerful garment night and day
> To God to pray who gave success
> That us He'd guard not us discard
> Give us reward and always bless

A pious couple, Beragh and Brig, brought to Patrick three lumps of cheese made of curds and also butter. 'Those are for the students.'

'Good indeed,' said Patrick. Thereupon a foreign druid, (Galldraoi) who had come to visit Patrick said, 'I'll believe in your religion if you turn these into stones.' Patrick did so. 'Now turn them into cheese again.' Patrick did so. 'Turn them once more into stones.' Patrick did so, but when the Galldraoi asked him to turn them back into cheese Patrick said, 'No. They shall remain for ever in commemoration of God's power and of your incredulity until shall come hither another servant of God to take charge of them.'

Then the Galldraoi believed.

Two of these stones stayed at Dichuill's oratory nearby and Dichuill took the other to Cluain Braoin (in Louth) when he became abbot, and the ancient author says it stands in Gort Copaich.

Bishop Fiac set up in Domhnach Fiac which Patrick had asked for from King Criffen. Patrick left of his familia to preach the Gospel in South Leinster, Mo Catog in Innis Fail, (beg Erin), Augustin in Innis Beg, Tecan, Diarmuid, Nainnidh, Paul, and Fellimy, great-grandson of Dubhthach.

Bishop Fiac remained there till sixty of his community died. Then an angel came to him and said, 'To the west of the River Barrow, in Cuil Maighe will be the place of your resurrection. The place in which they shall find the boar let it be where they will put the refectory, and the spot in which they will find the doe let it be there they will put the church.'

He was afraid to go there without the sanction of the king, and said he would not leave, even at an angel's bidding, without the sanction and authority of Patrick. Patrick, hearing of this, went to Fiac (from Armagh, late in Fiac's life) and marked out the site and See beyond the Barrow. He consecrated it and put his meeting house there, that is, he made it Fiac's cathedral church. King Criffen was buried here at Sletty when killed by Eochaidh Gunnat, his grandson. Patrick, at the suggestion of Saint Seachlann, sent his chariot and horses to Fiac. The first day, they went to Patrick's long-lived companion Saint Mochta in Louth, next day to Dunshaughlin where they were fed and they rested for three days, then to Killashee to Saint Auxilius, then to Manchan at Kilmonagh and were kept three nights, then to Sletty. Fiac was not willing to deprive Patrick of his means of transport but the horses kept going round the church of Fiac until the angel said to him, 'Patrick has sent them to thee on account of thy infirmity.' Fiac accepted them then. They had come without a driver.

Patrick spent seven years in Munster. He blessed the fort in Cashel and said that till doom only one slaughter would take place there (Inchiquin's, who was taken as a boy to England, reared there as a Protestant but who finally repented and left money to have Masses said for his soul).

Leaving his beloved Munster he went towards the Brosnacha river, but when the people of Munster got to know he was leaving them they hastened after him as if each of them would outstrip the others... whole households overtook him at the river and there was uttered a great shout of joy because they saw him once more (from this cheering the river is named).

Then, in the presence of all, he brought to life Fot, the son of Daragh, a youth aged twenty-seven. He fed the whole multitude at the river Craibhecha by blessing a bushel of corn which was given him by Bishop Trian, a pilgrim or missionary of the Romans, whence it was called the Feast of the Bushel. After that he blessed them once more, saying more or less as follows, but here we give it in verse in an ancient Irish metre but in English:

> A blessing on the Munster folk
> On ploughing yoke on fruiting tree
> On every crop to mountain top
> Where ever drop of dew shall be.

> God's blessing on their kitchen fire
> and may their byre be always full
> Be families great their count equate
> To sands that grate 'neath herring school.
>
> Great blessing on their hills and glens
> Their fields and pens their grass and wheat
> That fruit and fold feed young and old
> Let it be told good food they eat.

When Patrick was at Cruachan Crobhdhearg he instructed two daughters of Leary Eithne and Fedelma and before he baptised them he asked them, 'Do you believe that by baptism the sin of your father and mother (original sin) is taken away?'

'We believe it.'

'Do you believe in penance after sin?'

'We believe it.'

'Do you believe in life after death and a resurrection after judgement?'

'We believe it.'

'Do you believe in the unity of the church?'

'We believe it.'

Then he baptised them.

Patrick, Auxilius, Seachnall and Benignus decreed, 'If any very difficult question shall arise above the competence of the Irish clans it is to be referred to the See of Patrick, Archbishop of the Irish, and to the judgement of the Bishop of Armagh, but if he and his learned theologians cannot easily give a judgement we decree it is to be referred to the Apostolic See to the Chair of Peter, Bishop of Rome.

Bishop Iserninus knelt to Patrick on his own behalf and on behalf of his monastic familia and then received from Patrick his church and church lands recognising canonically Patrick's primacy and authority. He had not found success till he got Patrick's authorisation and blessing.

Patrick gave Brigid the veil when she was eighteen by the hands of Saint Mel and Saint Mac Caile at Saint Mac Caile's church on the south-eastern shoulder of Croghan Bri Eile. She is known as Saint Brigid of Kildare.

Patrick lived and worked through twenty-two years of Leary's reign, twenty years of Oilioll Molt's and he died in the nineteenth year of Lughaidh's reign, having in sixty-one years with masterly skill left Ireland and the Irish a Christian nation, living the Divine Life internally and externally. Saint Patrick got on well with King Leary internally transforming Ireland into what would soon be known as 'the island of saints and scholars', for the monasteries became powerhouses of knowledge (religious and secular) and they spread by teaching and example truth, virtue and grace throughout Europe where confusion had reigned after the Roman Empire began to collapse. Leary helped him to bring law and customs into harmony with divine law. King Lughaidh, overlooking what Patrick had done for him when a boy, began to smart under Patrick's prophesy that the descendants of Leary would not reign and started a campaign to destroy what he had done but was stopped by being killed by a stroke of lightning at Achad Forcai. Patrick, when the queen besought him not to curse her unborn child had said, 'I will not curse him till he opposes me.'

Twenty years after King Lughaidh had defeated Oilioll Molt in the Battle of Ocha, the two Loarns, the two Fearguses and the two Aonguses, six sons of Eochaidh Muinramhar, went to Scotland.

The Battle of Cill Osnach in Magh Fea, Co. Carlow was fought. Aongus son of Nadfraoch was killed and his wife Eithne Uathach by Mortach mac Earca and Oilioll, son of Dunluing. (He had reigned over Munster for thirty-six years.)

Fraoch son of Fionachuidhe, son of the king of Leinster, was killed in the Battle of Graine. Cairbre son of Niall fought the Battle of Eamhna (now Navan fort), and afterwards that of Ceann-Ailbhe in Leinster, also that of Seaghsa, where Duach Teangamhghadh, king of Connacht, was slain by Mortach Mac Earca. Duach had previously engaged in the battles of Dealga, Mochroma and of Tuama.

The people of Leinster fought the Battle of Loch Moighe against the Ui Neill wherein much blood was spilt on both sides.

Feargus Mor Mac Earca invaded Scotland.

In AD 493 Gelasius was Pope in the last year of Lughaidh who was succeeded by Mortoch son of Muireadhach, son of Eoghan, son of King Niall. His mother was Earca daughter of Loar (of Scotland).

In his reign, Saint Ciaran of Clonmacnoise was born. In one year he had to fight the battles of Cinnaich, Almhaine, Cliath, Eibhline and Magh Ailbhe. He died soon after Magh Ailbhe in the house of Ceitthigh. Near this time Ailbhe of Emly died and also the great Saint Brigid of Kildare, the Mary of the Gael, daughter of Dubhthaigh son of Dreimhne, Breasal, Deich, Connla, Art, Cairbre Niadh, Cormac, Aongus Mor, Eochaid Fion Fuathnairt, Feidlimidh Reachtmhar, son of Tuathal Teachtmhar.

Mortach reigned twenty-four years. In his sixth year Symmachus was elected Pope, in his twenty-first Hormisda was elected. About this time, Saint Colmcille was also born.

Tuathal Maolgarbh, son of Cormac Caoch, son of Cairbre, son of Niall succeeded. His mother was Comaoin daughter of Dall Bronuigh who hit his head against a stone.

In his reign of thirteen years Moctius (Mochta) died; he was a disciple of Saint Patrick and was aged three hundred years. Saint Baoithin was born. Comhgall king of Scotland died. Saint Mobhi died. He was called Bearcan also and was a prophet of the race of Fiachadh Baiceada, son of Cathair Mor. The Battle of Tortan was fought by the people of Leinster, and in it Earca, son of Oilioll Molt from whom came Firceara, lost his life.

Soon after, the Battle of Sligo was fought by the two young princes, Feargus and Domhnall, and in it Eoin Beal, who had ruled Connacht for thirty-five years was slain (said to be buried on Knoc na riogh, facing the Cinel Conail and Cinel Eoghain).

Saint Oghran of Leathruidh died; he was a descendant of Conaire son of Mogha Lamha. Saint Ciaran of Clonmacnoise died aged thirty-one. Bacach had his head struck off by Ciaran for swearing falsely, at the 'fair' of Tailtean in the sight of all.

Guaire took the kingship of Connacht after Eoin Beal. Eoin had a son Ceallach, a religious under Ciaran, and he let himself be persuaded to try for the kingship by leading a good body of forces who were intent on making him king. Ciaran soon missed him, cursed him fearfully and implored God to blast his design by sudden death. When Ceallach heard of this he returned in haste and prostrated himself and promised implicit obedience for the future and not to engage in anything without his consent. Ciaran imputing this to the folly of youth compassionately forgave him and blessed him but assured him his death was decreed to be violent and unexpected. He led an exemplary life after that and became a bishop but still wanted his younger brother to be king. However Guaire, by spies, found out the designs and preparations and considered things would not be safe while Ceallach was around, so he got the bishop's servants to kill him. Tuathal was slain by Maolmor son of Niathire at Greallagh Eille, at the request and instigation of his successor.

In AD 531 Diamuid, son of Feargus Ceirbheoil, son of Conal Creamthuine, son of King Niall. His mother was Corbhach, daughter of Maine (of Leinster).

In his reign Tighearnach bishop of Clones died. He was descended from Daire Barach son of Cathaoir Mor. Oilioll Mac Mortoch, king of Leinster for nine years, died.

Munster was ruled by Cormac son of Oilioll, Muireadhach, Eochaidh, Daire Cearb, Oilioll Flan Beg.

The Battle of Conaire at Ceara was fought by Feargus and Domhnal, sons of Mortoch mac Earca. In it, Oilioll Ionbhanda, king of Connacht, and his brother, Aodh Fortamhail, were slain. The Crom Chonuill plague overran the whole island and devastated the people and the monasteries. Mac Tuil of Cill Cuilin was carried off.

In the Battle of Cuill great numbers of Co. Cork were slain owing to the prayers of a pious lady; Suide Midhe, descended from Fiachadh Suidhe, son of Feidlimidh Reachtmhar. They had injuriously treated her and used her unbecoming her descent and character.

Eochaidh son of Connla, son of Caolbhadh, son of Cruin Badhraoi, king of Ulster died. Cormac son of Oilioll, king of Leinster, died, as did the prophet Beg Mac De, the bishop of Acha Cuingire, and Saint Neasin the leper.

Gawran king of Scotland died, and his foe Gruige son of Maolcion, king of the Picts, routed the Scots in a pitched battle. The Battle of Cul Dreimhne was fought between Feargus and Domhnall against this king, Diarmuid, over what they considered his improper treatment of their highly esteemed kinsman Saint Colmcille.

In AD 561 the Battle of Cooldrivne (now Cooladrumman) was fought. A copy of Saint Jerome's translation of the Vulgate copy of the Bible came to the monastery of Clonard in Co. Meath, and Saint Colm, knowing a good thing when he saw it, needed a copy of it for his own monasteries but failed to get it. So rising in the nights he copied it but the copy was demanded by the head of the monastery. Colm did not consider that just and went to the court of Diarmuid the High king for justice, but the king decided against him using the principle: 'to every cow its calf, to every book its copy.' At this Parliament of Tara the son of the king of Connacht killed someone (perhaps at hurling) and the law stood from of old that homicide was to be punished instantly by death for violence at the (Feis Teamhrach) convention of Tara. The boy knew this and fled for protection to two Northern princes, Fergus and Domhnal, who also knew the law and so for his safety gave him into the sanctuary-keeping of Colm – their kinsman. But he was pulled out and killed, and this was taken so badly that the clouds of war began to threaten. Diarmuid took his army thereafter to punish their insolence. The armies met between Ben Bulbin, Co. Sligo, and the sea, and Colm told all on his side not to go beyond a certain point – one disobeyed and was killed, and he was the only casualty on Fergus and Domhnall's side, but Diarmuid lost three thousand.

About two hours after the battle Colm went to the monastery of Ahamlish. Saint Molaise happened to be there visiting. He put the penance on Colm of going abroad and converting as many souls for Christ as were killed in the battle – but Colm had been involved in the Battles of Coolfey and Coleraine before Cool-Dreimhne. Diarmuid was defeated there and he was again defeated in the Battle of Cul Uinsion by Aodh Brenian king of Teabhtha. Very few of his men survived.

Colmcille was about forty-three years old when he went to Scotland. Soon after this the fight of Monadoire in the Highlands took place between Clanna Neill and seven petty kings of the Picts who were killed with most of their forces.

Colman Mor son of Cairbre, son of Dunluing, died after

ruling Leinster for thirty years. Sionach Cro, a nun, complained to Diarmuid that Guaire, king of Connacht, took her only cow. Diarmuid made war on him and beat him. Guaire was brave but his forces were very outnumbered and had to go on the run. When he met up with his generals it was decided to surrender unconditionally He was known and famed for his generosity, so Diarmuid gave him a few hard tests which proved beyond doubt that he was well-named Guaire the generous. Diarmuid admired him and they became friends.

Guaire's brother Saint Mochua retired with a priest to a spring of water south of Buirin to keep Lent with a very strict fast. The priest got terribly hungry on Easter morning before the saint had finished his devotions and asked leave to go to Guaire's court for some meat, as he was ready to drop with hunger. Mochua did not consider his request unreasonable but told him to be patient – that there would be no need for that journey. Guaire's meal was ready on the table, but he was amazed to see the dishes rise, leave the table and go towards Mochua. Disappointed at no dinner he ordered a body of horse to follow them, and he also followed. Seeing them, the priest was afraid of trouble, but Saint Mochua anchored the horses to the ground and made the riders immovable till the priest had finished a good meal. Then praying, he let them come. Guaire found him on his knees, knelt for his blessing and pardon, and the saint generously invited him and his retinue to have dinner with him. The five mile road is known as Bothair na Mias – Road of the Dishes.

Diarmuid's son Breasal took the fat cow of a religious woman who would neither sell nor exchange it for seven cows and a bull. He wanted it to feast his father at Kells in Meath. In the middle of the mirth the woman burst in and complained to the king, who was so enraged with Breasal that he ordered him to be drowned. He was drowned in the river Ruidhe.

Diarmuid repented this hasty killing of his son and applied himself to Saint Colmcille who advised him to go to Saint Beacan, and who went with him to plead his cause. When Saint Beacan saw it was the king of Ireland he cried out to him, 'O murderer, down onto the ground on your knees.'

Instantly, the king obeyed and at the urgent request of Colm,

Beacan prayed three times and restored Breasal to life, to the inexpressible joy of the king, who ever after held Saint in great veneration.

Saint Mochua wrote to Saint Colm in Iona the death-loss of the cock that used to waken him, the mouse that used to keep him awake and the fly that used to perch on the first word of the next sentence when he had fallen asleep or had to shut his tired eyes at his devotions – he took no more than five hours rest in twenty-four hours, and these were his only companions.

Colm received the news with Christian magnanimity comforting him in his reply, telling him he ought to mitigate his grief for these things, that his three companions were mortal and subject to the inexorable stroke of death and not to be surprised nor in an inordinate manner to lament their departure.

Diarmuid was slain by Aodh Dubh mac Suibhne at Rath Beg in Muighline and was buried at Cuinnirre. He was succeeded by Feargus and Domhnall, sons of Mortoch mac Earca and Duinseach, daughter of Duach Teangabha, king of Connacht.

These brothers governed without jealousy or dispute for one year. They had to fight the Battle of Gabhra Liffe against Leinster, wherein four hundred of the principal nobles and gentry of Leinster were slain together with the greater part of their army. Dioman mac Muireadhach, king of Ulster ten years, was slain by Bachlachuibb.

Feargus and Domhnall died and were succeeded by Eochaidh son of this Domhnall, and by Baodan his uncle, son of Mortoch. In their reign, Cairbre Crom son of Criffin Sreibh died (he had been king of Munster and had defeated Colman Beag son of Diarmuid in the Battle of Feimhin with terrible slaughter). Breandan Biorra, aged one hundred and eighty years, died. Fiachadh Baodan's son fought at Folla and Forthola against Ely and Ossory and won a complete victory by slaying incredible numbers.

Conull, leader of the Dalriada in Scotland, died. He was the son of Comhguill, and he bestowed Iona on Saint Colm.

Eochaidh and Baodan were slain by Crouan, son of Tighearnach of the Cianacht of Glen Geimhin (Dungivin), and they were succeeded by Ainmereach, son of Seadna, son of

Feargus Ceannfhada, son of Conal Gulban (Eiremhon's line). His royal consort was Bridget, daughter of Cobhtach from Ard Ladhran.

He was killed by Feargus MacNeill at Carraig Leime an Eich, and succeeded by Baodan, son of Nineadhadh, son of Feargus Ceannfhada. His royal consort was Cacht, daughter of Fionngall's king. In his reign, that lasted one year, the Battle of Bagha was fought. In it, Aodh son of Eochaidh Tiormcharnadh was killed. Cairbre Crom died, as did Baodan king of Ulster and Saint Ruadhan Lothra. This Baodan, the Ard-ri was treacherously slain by Cuimin son of Colman Beag, and by Cuimin son of Libhrein at Carraig Leime an Eich.

Aodh son of Ainmereach succeeded and reigned for twenty-seven years. He fought the Battle of Beallach Dathi, slew Colman Beag and five thousand of his troops.

In his reign the pious Seanach bishop of Clonard died; and Fiachadh son of Baodan, son of Muireadhach, who governed Ulster twenty-five years was killed by Fiachadh, son of Deamain, in the Battle of Beathadh. Feidlim king of Munster died.

Aodh summoned the Parliament or Convention of Drumceat (near Limavaddy), which lasted a year and a month, at which excellent laws were made for the correction of abuses and the prosperity of the people. The poets were not banished (as was intended) but reformed, and their state and numbers reduced, and they were put under the discipline of excellence, their chief being Dallan Forgaill, alias Eochaidh Eigeas (Eochaidh the learned). When Colm was defending the bards he said, 'The great Patrick pressed Ossian to reel out the stories of the Fianna.'

The bards were saved by Saint Colmcille who miraculously punished the queen and her maid and the king's son whom he cursed and caused twenty-seven bells to be rung against, corresponding to the twenty-seven he had led astray into the dishonouring of the clergy. Conal was his name, and is known as Conal Clogach (of the bells). Conal lost his reason and his estate and the succession, and the king's other son gave love, honour and religious respect to the saint, and received the blessings and prosperity and the throne that Colm asked God for.

Aodh refused to release Scanlon son of the king of Ossery at the saint's request, so when Colm was going away he visited the Dubh Regles in Derry where Scanlon was confined with oppression. The night after he arrived a large tower of fire and light appeared in the air over where Scanlon was. The soldiers fell flat on the ground astonished at the bright terrible fiery appearance. Night was like midday and a ray of light lit up the castle's building and darted into Scanlon's cell. A voice called him, 'Stand up, Scanlon, leave your chains and fetters behind you.' The angel led him out and answered the soldiers: 'Scanlon the king of Ossery is delivered from his imprisonment.'

The king was presented to Saint Colm, but was unable to speak from thirst and the effect of salt meat on his throat. The saint told Baoithin to give him a large bowl of water – which he finished in three draughts and regained his speech. Colm told him to resume the government, not to fear Aodh, and to assure him he gave him his Episcopal staff, telling him to leave it at the monastery of Armuigh (in Ossery).

King Aodh would not grant freedom from tribute to the Gaels of Scotland even at the urgent request of Colm not to send an army there to impose it. Saint Colm warned him that providence had taken that illustrious clan under special protection and was able to defend it – as happened. Aodhan (Ian) son of Gabhran son of Domhanguirt was in Saint Colm's retinue.

Saint Colm never again beheld Ireland, as a penance for his part or his occasioning the bloody engagements of Cul Dreimhne.

Cul Rathain had been between Dalnaruidhe and Ulster (Ulster then is County Down today), over an insult to Colm by Comhgall, Cull Feadha against Colman son of Diarmuid, in defence of his son Colman who was implicated in the slaying of Baodan the nephew of Colm, and who had been Ard-ri for one year.

To Drumceat, Colm was accompanied, by twenty bishops, forty priests, fifty deacons and thirty students of divinity.

Among those present were Criomhthan king of Leinster, Iollan son of Scanlon, Maolduin king of West Munster, Guaire king of Clan Fiachadh north and south, Fingin king of Munster, Criomhthan king of West of Ireland, Raghallach king of Tuatha Taighdean, Ceallach king of Breffney-O'Reilly, Congallach

Ceannmaghuir king of Tir Conail, Fearguil king of Ailtheach, Guaire son of Conguill king of Ulster, the two kings of Oriel, Daimin son of Aongus (from Colchar Deasa to Fionn Carn at Sliabh Fuaid), and Aodh son of Duach Gallach (from Fionn Carn to the Boyne).

In the reign of Aodh, Saint Caineach of Achad Both died. The Battle of Sleamhna was won by Colman Rimidh, in which Aodh and his son Conall and their army were defeated; the Battle of Cuill Caol was fought in which Fiachadh son of Deamain was routed by Fiachadh mac Baodan. Conall son of Suibhne won the three battles of Bruighin Da Choga, in one day defeating Aodh Slaine, Aodh Buidhe and Aodh Roinn. Aodh the Ard-ri was slain in the Battle of Beallach Duin Bolg.

Aodh Slaine seized the government and reigned for six years. He was a son of Diarmuid. He admitted as partner in the government Colman Rimidh son of Mortach mac Earca.

Aodh's mother was Mungan daughter of Congearuinn Mac Duaigh. He married Eithne, daughter of Breannuin Dall, both from Connacht.

In their reign Pope Gregory (590–604) deputed Saint Augustine to convert England. Colman was slain by Lochan Diolmhain, and Aodh was slain by Conal Guthbhin.

They were succeeded for twenty-seven years by Aodh Uairiodhnach son of Domhnal, son of Mortach mac Earca. His mother was Bridget daughter of Orca, Eiric and Eachach. He suffered from appendicitis (whence his name) but could endure the fatigues of war. His reign was often disturbed by Aongus son of Colman whom he finally defeated in the bloody Battle of Odhbha (Navan). In it, Conal Laoghbreagh was also slain (he was a son of Aodh Slaine). This king, Aodh was killed in the Battle of Da Fearta, and was succeeded by Maolchobha son of Aodh, Ainmereach, Seadna, Feargus Ceannfhada son of Conall Gulban (Eiremhon's line). His wife was Craoiseach daughter of Aodh Fionn king of Ossery. He fell by the sword of his successor in the dreadful Battle of Bulgadan after a reign of four years.

In AD 622 Suibhne Meann son of Fiachra, Fearadhach, Mortach, Muireadhach, Eoghan and Niall (Eiremhon's line).

In his reign Saint Kevin of Glen Da Loch died aged one

hundred and twenty years. He was of the posterity of Labhra Loingseach. He it was who petrified Caineog and her companion when they had reached the hill above the glen on their way to kill a child. Saint Adhamhnan (Eunan), son of Ronan, Tinne, Aodh, Colm, Seadna, Feargus, Conal Gulban, son of King Niall was born in this king's reign.

Suibhne's wife was Rona, daughter of the king of Ui Durtri.

He was slain by Conall Claon son of Scanlon Sgiath Leathan after thirteen years and succeeded by Domhnal.

In AD 635 Domhnal son of Aodh mac Ainmereach (Eiremhon's line). He routed Conall Claon after dreadful slaughter at Dun Citherne.

In his reign Saint Fiontan, alias Munna, who owned the book Saint Colmcille copied, died, also Saint Mochua, and Molaise the pious bishop of Leithglin.

Saint Mochuda, alias Carthach, founded Rahan where he had seven hundred and ten religious. One of these, a lay monk, was a Pictish nobleman, very big and strong, whose name was Constantine, obtained two years respite for the abbot and monks who were being expelled from Rahan for unworthy motives, but he died before he could get a third year. Those who acted in an unworthy way in the expulsion Saint Mochuda cursed and asked heaven to punish the family of Blathmac son of Aodh Slaine, who led the rabble and rough-handled Saint Mochuda and his company.

Diarmuid, a brother of Blathmac, was reverent towards the saint and would not lay impious hands on him or on his religious or on the sick or maimed and when he returned to Blathmac he was scoffed at as the saint had told him, but the saint assured him of blessings and honour on him and on his posterity and the name 'Ruaighnigh' (Rooney) would be a name of distinction to him and his posterity.

The king of the Decies gave the saint honourable protection and a place to build a monastery at Lismore. He performed many miracles.

In Domhnal's reign the Battle of Muighrath was fought in which Conall Claon (ten years king of Ulster) was slain.

Saint Mochua died, (he was a descendant of Cathaoir Mor), as did Saints Mochuda, Molaise, Comhdan mac Da Cearda and Cronan, bishop of Caoindrom.

Domhnal died a natural death and was succeeded by Conal Caol and his brother Ceallach, sons of Maolchabha, Aodh, Ainmereach, Seadna, Feargus Ceannfhada and Conal Gulban. They reigned in peace and unanimity for thirteen years.

In their reign Raghallach son of Uadhach, who had ruled Connacht for twenty-five years, killed his nephew treacherously. Having learned from a draoi that their next child would be the occasion of punishment from heaven, he gave orders to have it given to a swineherd to be destroyed. It was put naked in a bag, but the man was so moved by its cries and its beauty and sweet face that he took it to a religious woman and hung the bag on a cross in full view of her cell. He came home by a hidden way and the nun, who had been out, soon returned and educated it at her own expense. The little girl became famous for her beauty and personality and Raghallach took her by force when the nun refused to give her and he retained her at the expense of her character. His wife asked the help of the church, and Feicin Fabhair attended with divines and religious persons of several orders, but was not successful in turning Raghallach from his sinful way. They left the court and implored the justice of heaven to overtake the king not to let him live till the following May, to use despicable weapons and the meanest people, and to let him die in a place unbecoming the majesty of a king, and end his days in a vile and ignominious manner.

He wounded a stag with a spear on an island and followed it, only to find rustics cutting it up. He demanded it from them in an angry tone. They had agreed to divide it among themselves. As they saw the king had only a few wet followers they fell to them with their turf-spades and killed him, having knocked him off his horse, and they killed most of his retinue.

Marron, the queen, died soon after, as did the daughter. In Conal Caol's reign Diarmuid Ruaighnigh won the Battle of Carn Conuill in which Cuan Conuill king of the Figinte and Cuan, son of Amholgadhg, king of Munster ten years, and Talmonach, king of Ui Liathain, were slain. We are told he obtained this victory at the incessant prayer of the religious of Clonmacnois, for which he showed great gratitude. He settled the estate of Liathmhantan on the abbey and ordered his body to be buried there.

The nun Saint Fursa, who was of the posterity of Lughaidh Laga, died. Cuana son of Cailchine king of Fearney in South Munster died. He was like Guaire who excelled in munificence and charity and was called the renowned champion of Liathmuine.

Saint Mocheallog of Kilmallock, who was descended from Conaire son of Eidersgeol, died. Ceallach was lost at Brugh-Os-Boinn, and Conal was slain by Diarmuid Ruaighnaigh.

In AD 661 Blathmac and Diarmuid Ruaighnaigh, sons of Aodh Slaine, seized the throne.

In their reign the Battle of Puncty was fought, in which the king of England and thirty of his principal nobles were slain. The Irish historians record this contemporaneous battle which happened in the reign of these two kings, but the Irish were not involved.

Saint Oltan and Moaodhog (Mogue), who built the monasteries of Fearna, Rosinver and Drumlane both died. Cuimin Fada the monk son of Fiachradh, and Saint Mannach son of Fingin, king of Munster died. The dreadful plague called the Buidhe Chonuill carried off both kings.

In AD 668 Seachnusach son of Blathmac of Eiremhon's line succeeded and reigned for six years. In his reign the Battle of Feirt was fought between Ulster and the Picts with terrible slaughter on both sides. Baothin, abbot of Beanchuir, died.

The king was killed by Dubh Duin of the Cinel (clan) Cairbre and succeeded by Cionnfhaola son of Blathmac, who reigned four years.

In his reign invading foreigners burned to the ground the Monastery of Beannchuir. The name Beannchuir dates from the time Breasal Breac took a big army to Scotland and successfully returned with a large booty of horned cattle, many of which he killed. Their horns were scattered around the place where his camp was and where his victorious army feasted for some time (beanna means horns). When Saint Comhgall built his monastery here he retained the old name.

Cionnfhaola was killed in the Battle of Cealtrach by his

successor.

In AD 678 Fiannachta Fleadhach (the festive), son of Dunchadha, son of Aodh Slaine of Eiremhon's line, ruled seven years. The Venerable Bede (this title was given by angels), relates that invaders from Wales (or rather Cambria), led by their principal commanders, did cruel devastations on the Irish, and he also asserts that in AD 684 the forces of the king of England (Lagria) under a General Bertus miserably ravished that innocent nation which was a most friendly ally to the English. In this invasion was fought the Battle of Rathmor at Maigh Glinne in which Cumasgach king of the Picts and many Irish were slain. These Welsh transported themselves from there to the Isles of Orcades which they plundered without mercy. Some of these Welsh landed on the north coast of Leinster and spoiled the inhabitants with great cruelty, sparing none and robbing churches.

In this reign Colman, the pious bishop of Inis Bo Finne, died. Saint Fionnan, who blessed Ard-Fionnan and who was of the posterity of Fiachadh Muilleathan, and Saint Aranan also died.

This king fought the Battle of Lochgabhair wherein many of the Leinster people were slain.

The learned man Cionn-Faola died and in the same year Dungall, son of Scanlan, king of the Picts, and Cionnfaola king of the Ciannacht of Glen-Givin were buried by Maolduin son of Maolfithrigh at Dun Ceitrin.

Fiannachta, the king, was killed by Aodh son of Dubhthaigh and by Conning at Greallach Dolling after a reign of seven years.

In AD 685 Loingseach son of Aongus, Domhnall, Aodh, Ainmerach, of the line of Eiremhon reigned for eight years. The meaning of Loingseach is mariner or an admiral of a fleet; in English: Lynch.

In his reign Saint Eunan, ninth abbot of Iona, came to Ireland to propagate the faith among the Irish. Saint Moling Lauchradh died, the Welsh invaded and plundered dreadfully Magh (Muirteimhne) Muirtheimhne around Dundalk. A dreadful cattle disease raged in Ireland and in England for three years, causing a dreadful famine in both countries, and it was reported that human flesh was eaten. Saint Egbert undertook to preach the Gospel in Scotland.

The Ulster people engaged the Welsh in the Battle of Magh Cuillin and slew almost their whole army. Eunan (Adamhnan), ninth abbot of Iona, who wrote a life of Saint Colmcille, still extant, died aged seventy-seven years.

The Saracens invaded the Grecian Empire in terrible numbers, besieged Constantinople for three years but failed to take it. The pious bishop of Ardfert Coimhdhean died, and soon after the Battle of Cormin was fought by Ceallach son of Raghallach in which bloody engagement Loingseach lost his throne.

In AD 693 Congal Cionnmaghair succeeded. He was a son of Feargus Fanuid of the race of Conal Gulban, son of King Niall. He was a cruel persecutor of the church and burned the regular and secular clergy without mercy or distinction at Kildare. He died suddenly and unlamented. He reigned nine years.

In AD 702 Feargall, son of Maolduin, son of Maolfithrigh, son of Aodh Uairiodnach succeeded and reigned seventeen years. His mother was Cacht, daughter of Maolchabha, king of Cinel Conuill.

In his reign Bishop Baodan of Innis Bo Finne died. The Battle of Cloch Minuire, with equal slaughter on both sides for part of the day, was won by the bravery of the Dalriadas over the Welsh, with the loss of most of their army.

Neachtan, king of Scotland, expelled a convent of monks who reprehended his conduct thereby causing discontent among his subjects.

A wonderful event took place during Feargall's reign. Three showers fell, one of honey at Foithin Beag, one of silver (airgid) at Foithin Mor, and one of blood at Magh Laighion (a shower like blood is not unknown in northern regions when a red dust gets into the atmosphere).

The Battle of Almhuinne between Feargall and Morough Mac Broin king of Leinster was fought. Feargall had twenty-one thousand troops, Morough had nine thousand plus eighty-nine champions and his household troops.

The battle was desperate. Feargall had to give way, three thousand three hundred of his men were slain. At the first onset terror seized his men, a dreadful apparition hung in the air over them so that even those who escaped were distracted, and about a third of his army was lost.

Some of his forces had, on their march, broken into the church of Cillin and took all the holy vessels, and a cow of a hermit. This pious old man laid dreadful imprecations on the king and asked God for exemplary vengeance on Feargall and on his army. He was killed with the defeat of his sacrilegious forces.

In AD 719 Fogartach son of Niall, son of Cearmuig, son of Sotuill, son of Diarmuid, son of Aodh Slaine (Eiremhon's line) reigned but one year, and lost his life by Cionaoith, son of Iargallach, in the Battle of Beilge, and he succeeded him.

In AD 720 Cionaoith son of Iargallach, Conuing Carraig, Congaille, Aodh Slaine of Eiremhon's line.

In Cionaoith's reign the Reliquary of Eunan (Adhamhnan) was brought to Ireland.

It contained a lock of the Blessed Virgin's hair, the loin cloth used on Calvary, Saint Bridget's hair-shirt, a tooth of Saint Declan of Ardmor, a bone of Fingin Cam, part of the cloak Saint Martin gave the beggar, the inner garment of the Blessed Mother of God, the books of John the pure and the cloak of Saint Enda of Arran and other things.

In the Battle of Drum Curran the army of Cionaoith was defeated, and he was found dead on the field. He had reigned four years.

In AD 724 Flaithbheartach son of Loingseach, Aongus, Domhnal, Aodh and Ainmereach succeeded, being victorious. His mother was Murion, daughter of Ceallach.

In his reign the Battle of Drom Dearg in Scotland was fought between two brothers, sons of Aongus, king of the Picts. The succession to the throne was settled by the defeat and death of Drust and the victory of Aongus Mac Aongusa.

The Battle of Murbuilg in Scotland was fought soon afterwards between the Picts and the Dalriada. The Picts were defeated with great slaughter. The Battle of Fotharta in Muirtheimhne was fought between Aodh Ollan (Clanna Neill) and the Ulster people. Aodh Roin, king of Ulster thirty years, was slain, also Concha, son of Cuanach, king of Cobha.

Not long after this Loingseach, who had been king of Ireland, died a natural death at Armagh after Flaithbheartach, his son, held the throne for seven years.

In AD 731 Aodh Ollan (Allan) got possession, son of Feargall, Maolduin, Maolfithrigh and Aodh Uairiodnach (Eiremhon's line) and reigned nine years. His mother was Bridget daughter of Orca, son of Carrthon. In his reign Munster and Leinster fought the Battle of Beallach Faile in which many fell on both sides. Ceallach, son of Faobhuir king of Ossery, was killed. Victory was long doubtful, but at last Cathall son of Fionguine won.

Aongus son of Feargus, king of the Picts, made a devastating incursion into the Dalriada. He took Dungal and Feargus, sons of Sealbhaigh, prisoners, burned and levelled Dun Greidhe, and his cruelties were a terror to all.

Aodh and Cathall, sons of Fionguine, consulted together how and by what measures they could advance the revenue of Saint Patrick throughout the kingdom, and so they legislated.

The Battle of Athseanuigh was fought between Aodh and Aodh, son of Colgan, king of Leinster, who was slain, and Aodh Allan was dangerously wounded. About nine thousand of the Leinster people were slain, and also many of the Ard-ri's men, together with Aodh son of Mortoch, who shared the throne with Aodh Allan.

Flann son of Cronmaol the pious and charitable bishop of Rotheruine died and also Cathall king of Munster and the martial prince Aodh Balbh, seven years king of Connacht.

Aodh Allan was slain in the Battle of Seiridhmidh (near Ceananus) by Morrough.

In AD 740 Domhnal son of Morrough, Diarmuid, Airmeadh Caoch, Conall Guithbhin, Suibhne, Colman Mor, Feargus Ceirbheoil, Conal Creamhthuine and King Niall got the throne of Ireland for forty-two years.

His mother was Ailpin daughter of Congall of Dealbhna Mor. In his reign Colman, bishop of Laosan, was killed by O'Durraire. Cormac bishop of Ath Trim died; a monstrous serpent was seen moving in the air; after which Seachnusach son of Colgan, king of Ui Kinsalach, died and soon Cathasach son of Oilioll, king of the Picts, was killed at Rath Beatach by the people of Leinster. Suarleach, bishop of Fabhair, and Osbran, bishop of Cluan Creamha, eminent prelates, died.

The Battle of Beallach Cro was fought by Criffin, son of Eana, in which Finn, son of Airb king of Dealbhna, was slain with great numbers of his army. From the dreadful slaughter the lake near Tobur Fionn got the name Loch Beallin Cro (blood). Cumusgach, king of Offaly, was killed by Maolduin, son of Aodh Beanain, king of Munster.

Aongus, king of Scotland, resigned his crown and his life. Dungall and many Leinster nobles lost their lives in the Battle of Beallach Gabhra. It was fought by Maconceara and the people of Ossery against Dungall, son of Laidhgin of the Ui Cinnsalach.

Soon Mortoch, son of Murchadh king of Leinster, died. Domhnal the Ard-ri died from natural causes, and was succeeded by Niall Freasach.

In AD 782 Niall Freasach (born about the time of the showers of honey, silver and blood) son of Feargall, son of Maolduin reigned for four years. His mother was Aithiochta, daughter of Cein O'Conner king of the Cianachta of Glengivin.

In his reign Dubhionrachtach son of Cathall, son of Muireadhach Muilleathan, five years king of Connacht, died. Many terrible earthquakes in several parts of Ireland took place.

A most miserable famine destroyed multitudes. Dungall son of Ceallach king of Ossery died, also Cronmaol the pious bishop of Kilmore, Ailpin king of the Picts, and Colgnait the charitable bishop of Ardbraccan.

The Battle of Acha Liag between the Ui Bruin and the Ui Maine was sharp and concluded with great slaughter on both sides.

Shortly after the battle, Artgoile went on pilgrimage to Iona, and Feargus, bishop of Damliag, died. The fierce Battle of Corran was fought between the Cinel Connuill and the Cinel Eoghan. The Siol Eoghain under Aodh Allan, king of Fochla, won, defeating Domhnal son of Aodh Muindearg with great loss and the rout of his whole army.

King Niall died in Iona shortly after this, and was succeeded by Donchadha, son of Domhnal, Murchadh, Diarmuid, Airmeadh Caoch, Conull Guthbhin; Suibhne, Colman Mor, Feargus Ceirbheoil, Conall Creamhthuine and Niall of the nine hostages.

He died in his own bed after a reign of twenty-seven years.

In AD 813 Aodh Dorndighe son of Niall Frasach succeeded. His mother was Dunfhlaith daughter of Flaithbheartach son of Loingseach king of the Cinel Conuil.

When weaned he began to suck his fingers, from whence his name.

In his reign the Danes first landed in west Munster with fifty sail and a numerous army. Airtree, a descendant of Heber Finn king of Munster, led a strong army against them. In a desperate battle the Danes fled in confusion, leaving four hundred and sixteen of their men dead. Only because of darkness coming on were more of them able to escape.

Six years later when Feidlimidh was king of Munster another fleet (from Norway) landed on the coast of Munster and plundered and ravaged with barbarity.

The Irish repulsed them with great slaughter and chased them out of Munster. In the seventh year of Aodh's reign the tyrant Turgil, son of the king of Norway, made an attempt on the kingdom. Olchabhair was king of Munster (son of Cionnfhaoith, Congall, Maolduin and Aodh Beanain).

The Danes are called Dubhgeinte and Dubhlochlannaigh. The Norwegians are called Fionngeinte and Fionn Lochlannaigh. Lochlannach means a person strong or powerful at sea.

Their sixty ships landed many troops at Caomh Inis Obhrathadh and they plundered and burned with dreadful cruelty at Inis Labhraine, Dairinis, and coastal parts.

They made another descent on Ireland in the second year of Feidlimidh king of Munster and with their cruel barbarities ravaged and burned Inis Eibhin, Beannchur, Cluain Umhadh, Ros Maoileadh and Sgeilg Mhichil.

Another fleet landed in the east about the same time, ravaging Beannchuir, Co. Down with fire and sword. They killed its bishop and its religious, and they broke open the rich shrine of Saint Comhgall. Another fleet reinforced them and landed at Ui Cinnsallach. These Norwegians terrorised the natives, who fled for their lives, and so they plundered Teach Munna, Teach Moling, and Inis Tiog. They then began to spoil and pillage Ossery, but Ossery bravely mustered and slew seven hundred and seven of them and gave them a complete defeat, but the others continued as usual; plundering and devastating.

They plundered Dundergmuighe, Inis Eoghain, Diosiort, Tiobruid and Liosmor.

They ransacked and burned Cill Molaise, Glendaloch, Cluain Ard, Mobheodhg, Suird Colmcill, Damhliag-Ciaran, Slaine, Cealla Saile, and Cluain Uadhme Mungairid. Churches were stripped and burned, as were most of the monasteries.

Another fleet landed at Limerick and Corcabaisgin; Tradhruighe, and Ui Conuill Gabhra were burned but Ui Conuill routed them at Seanuid and took back the spoil from them.

Turgil, with a large fleet, landed in the north and had many men with him. He united the rest with him and determined to conquer the whole country. He secured what the foreigners held, and they received him with joyful acclamations and united under him as their general and began hostilities to conquer the country.

He sent many of his troops to conquer Leath Cuinn. He divided his fleet, sending some to Loch Neachach, others to Lughmhaigh and others to Loch Ribh, with orders to ravage with fire and sword, spare none, de-spirit the people by cruelty and terror and take possession in security. These instructions were obeyed.

Armagh was plundered three times in a month, its abbot taken prisoner as Saint Colmcille foretold when he said, 'The most religious abbot of Armagh shall, by force of Norwegian arms, be seized and made a prisoner of war.'

It had been predicted by some ecclesiastics that the sins of the nobility and people would be punished by very terrible visitations which would overrun the land in the reign of Aodh Dorndighe and Artre.

Turgil fixed himself in the church and its estates in Armagh and kept these till he was drowned by Maolseachlann in Loch Ainnin. Inis Patrick suffered the common calamities as did most of the islands between Ireland and Scotland.

Iona fell to them and they invaded Scotland with their cruelty and barbarity.

Aodh Dorndighe, under provocation, invaded the province of Leinster, plundered for a month and slew many on his way to Dun Cuair, and divided that province equally between

Muireadhach, son of Ruarach and Muireadhach, son of Bruin.

About a year after this, in the second half of March, there were terrible peals of thunder, and the lightning destroyed a thousand and ten men and women between Corcabaisgin near the mouth of the Shannon in Co. Clare and the seaside, while at the same time the sea invaded in a dreadful manner and added to its channel land sufficient to graze twelve cows – never to be recovered. The tempest raged, and the current of water was so violent that it cut the island called Inis Fidhe in three parts.

Muireadhaig monastery was plundered and burned and spoiled in Omhaill, north of Clew bay, Co. Mayo.

Eochaidh bishop of Tamhleacht died as did Eidersgoil son of Ceallach, the pious prelate of Glendaloch and Siadhuall, the good bishop of Roscommon.

In AD 837 Aodh, after twenty-four years troubled reign was killed at Moigh Conuille in the Battle of Da Fearta by Maolcanaigh and succeeded by Conchobhar (Connor) son of Donoch, Domhnal, Murchadh, Diarmuid and Airmeadh Caoch of Eiremhon's line.

In his reign the most exemplary bishop of Athtrim, Cionfhaola, died and soon after that Eochaidh O'Tuathail, bishop of Luigh Moigh.

Inis Damhlaig and Cork were plundered, as were Dun-da-leith-glas (Downpatrick), and Moigh Bhille (Moville in Co. Down). They burned Moigh Bhille, having enclosed its hermits and burned them.

The Battle of the Plain of Tailtion was fought by Connor against the Gailiongach, who lost many. The Gailiongach were Firbolgs who were expelled from Scottish islands by the Picts and got territory in Leinster from King Caibre Niafer who oppressed them with taxes so they went to Queen Maeve and settled in Connacht.

The Leinster people mustered and fought the foreigners at Drum Conla. Much blood was spilt and victory was doubtful for some time till the Leinster troops gave ground and were pursued with terrible slaughter.

The valiant Conuing son of Conchoingiolt, chief of the Fothartuath, a Leinster district, was slain in this battle.

Armagh was plundered by the victorious foreigners with great barbarity, and in the following month they spoiled Lughmhagh, Finne Chianachta and Liosmor and all the churches they met, killing, expelling and taking the valuables and the sacred things as booty.

They wrecked the universities of Dun-da-leith-glas, Liosmor and Cashel and many lesser places of learning. An old roll discovered in the library of Oxford records seven thousand students attending the University of Armagh prior to the coming of the Danes.

Conchobhar, hopeless and helpless, is said to have died of grief after fourteen years on the very troubled throne of Ireland.

In AD 851, Niall Caille, son of Aodh Dorndighe, son of Niall Frasach succeeded, and he tried to hold the throne for fifteen years. His mother was Meidhbh daughter of Ionrachtach, son of Muireadhach king of Duirlus.

In his reign the foreigners plundered Loch Bricirne, and killed Congallach son of Neachach. They plundered Fearna Moaodhog (Mogue) Mungairid and Iollar Ceall (in Ormond). Churches and monasteries were rifled and demolished, the religious expelled with unheard-of violence, and the magnificent church of Kildare was destroyed.

Their success encouraged the Normans to try also. With a number of transports they landed at the Boyne, and with forty sail entered the Liffey. These are said to have exceeded the Norwegian foreigners in hostilities and rapine.

The Lochlannaigh (Norwegians, Danes, and people from regions around the Baltic) were alarmed and feared the Normans would join with the Irish and drive them out of Ireland, so they gathered their forces and gave battle.

The fight began briskly and there was dreadful slaughter on both sides, but the Lochlannaigh won and pursued the Normans from Inbhir na mBarc where the battle was fought, along the banks of the Shannon to the seaside. The victory animated them; they burned Inis Cealtrach, Cluain Mac Nois and the churches of Loch Eirne, once they had ransacked them as usual.

Feidlimidh the ecclesiastical prince, son of Criomhthan, king of Munster for twenty-seven years under provocation sorely distressed and plundered from Birr to Tara where he overcame some opposition. He lost his life in battle against Ionrachtach son of Maolduin.

Olochobhair abbot of Imly had himself elected king of Cashel. (Imly was the headquarters of the Martins, a pre-Gaelic tribe.)

Maolseachlann, king of Meath, slew seven hundred of the Lochlannaigh at Casan Linge. Saxolb, a general of theirs, was killed by the Cianacht and many of their troops. They were also defeated at Eas Aodha Ruaidh (Assaroe on the Earne) where many of them were slain.

Recovering somewhat, they took Dublin with the sword. Exnich the pious bishop of Teilge was unfortunately killed. The Connacht people tried to oppose them but were beaten and Maolduin son of Muirghuisa was slain with many of them. Another fleet arrived at Lough Neagh, plundered, destroyed, burned and killed. They burned Fearns and Cork. Niall plundered and destroyed Fearceall and Dealbhna Eathra; soon after, Morroch son of Aodh, king of Connacht, died.

The Lochlannaigh erected a fort at Linn Duachaill which they filled with their best troops. They plundered and destroyed Tuatha Teabhtha. They also built another castle at Dublin from where they had opportunities of ruining Leinster and Ui Neill. Churches were levelled and the country distressed from Dublin to Sliabh Bladhma. They ransacked Cluain Aidnach, Cluain Ioraird and Cluain Mac Nois and the land became like an uninhabited wilderness. Turgil erected a fort at Loch Ribh and from there they plundered Cluain Fearta Breanuin, Tir Da Glas and Lothra, as well as many other places. Muireadhach, bishop of Laine Leire, died.

Niall defeated the Lochlannaigh in Co. Armagh, killed numbers of them, put the rest to flight and followed them to the Callan river, which was swollen by heavy rain. He commanded a horseman to try the ford, but he was washed away. He commanded others to save him but they hesitated. Intent on saving him he rode to the very brink preparing to jump in but the bank gave way under the horse and both fell in and the king was drowned. (It had been predicted that he would be drowned in that stream, whence his historical identification name to distinguish him from other Nialls.)

In AD 866 Turgil, son of the king of Norway, was proclaimed king by the foreigners and great numbers of them poured into the country.

Saint Comcille foretold the calamities that would befall the Irish nation, and Saint Bearcan the prophet predicted, 'The bold Norwegians with numerous sail shall try the Irish Ocean and arrive upon the coasts. The isle shall be enslaved by these victorious foreigners. In every church an abbot of their own they shall place and shall proclaim a king of the Norwegian race to fill the throne of Ireland.'

Turgil ruled with a rod of iron and the Gaels were forced to taste the very dregs of servitude though they had often defeated and slain many of them. Olchobhair king of Munster with Lorcan king of Leinster killed Tomair, heir to the throne of Denmark with twelve hundred of his best troops. Five hundred were killed near Cashel. Many were killed by Tir-Conail. The Ui Fighinte killed three hundred and sixty, the Cianacht destroyed two hundred, Tighernach killed two hundred and forty at Drum Da Chon and Maolseachlann slew seventeen hundred at Glasglean.

Yet they were far from being suppressed, for they were getting fresh recruits from their own lands.

Turgil covered Ireland with petty kings, put his captains in districts, his abbots in the churches and monasteries and his sergeants in villages. His soldiers he billeted in houses and cottages with full powers over the owner and his property. The insolence and rapine of these were insupportable, as were their sordid and cruel tempers, and they could bring the Irish to their army rendezvous, where they could be confined in the guardroom till the soldier brought about the ruin of their families and fortunes.

They were not suffered to have their children taught, public worship was not allowed, needlework and embroidery in gold, silver or silk were forbidden to girls, boys were not permitted to learn the use of arms nor of martial arts, no public entertainments nor hospitality for the Irish – but they themselves indulged their palates and amused themselves in scandalous and unnatural debauch.

The Irish clergy, in bogs and caves, strictly performed the divine office of the church as best they could; they fasted and prayed and they obliged the laity to do likewise and beseech God for redemption and for the restoration of liberty to the kingdom and for the destruction of the power of the enemies of man and of God's church.

And God did this. Turgil built a palace near that of Maolseachlann, who governed Meath. He asked Maolseachlann for his daughter, promising to make her head of the women. Maolseachlann persuaded him in a reasonable way that things would have to be done secretly to preserve the honour of this nice girl and he pointed out to Turgil a better way of doing things. A time was arranged and she was to be accompanied by fifteen beauties even nicer than her (note here that 'her' is the disjunctive form of the pronoun). This seemed fine to Turgil. It happened that there was a convention of the Lochlannaigh in Dublin, so when all was settled to his satisfaction he invited fifteen of his chiefs and favourites to this feast. Maolseachlann got fifteen virtuous and beautifully featured boys, dressed them as girls, and instructed them how to conceal their knives, and what to do with them at the proper time and to preserve the honour of his daughter at all costs. These beardless boys had great hope of success and their hope was wedded to the ardent desire of freeing the Gaels. Maolseachlann came secretly and awaited the arranged signal beneath the castle walls with some well-chosen men who knew their part.

All went as planned. Turgil, with a knife to his throat, kept silent, the rest of the 'girls' slew their men as ordered, and Maolseachlann finished the work with his warriors. Word soon spread through Ireland... the Lochlannaigh fled to their ships, fortresses, bogs – anywhere.

The Irish, with wrongs boiling their battle-fury, hunted them out of all places and slew with fury great multitudes of them before they could reach their ships.

The king of Meath, seeing those who asked for mercy and surrendered their arms might be useful, spared them. The 'girls' tied up Turgil, and Maolseachlann upbraided him with great rebuke for his misdeeds and cruelty, and afterwards drowned him.

He had held the kingship over the freedom-loving Gaels for thirteen years. Loch Ainnin, wherein he was drowned, takes its name from a son of Nevy whose grandson Briotan Maol is the ancestor of the Britains.

In AD 879 Maolseachlann, for overcoming Ireland's torturers, was elected Ard-ri. He is the first of that name to be elected Ard-ri. Son of Donoch, Domhnal, Murchadh, Diarmuid, Airmeadh Caoch, Conall Guthbhin, Suibhne Meann, Colman Mor, Diarmuid and Feargus Ceirbheoil (of Eiremhon's line), he reigned for sixteen years. His mother was Arog daughter of Cathall, son of Fiachradh king of Bearchuil.

The Lochlannaigh, being driven out after they had tasted a riotous and expensive way of life, found the change not to their liking and concerted plans for a return. They sent three persons from Norway as peaceable merchants but they were officers and obtained settlements which they gradually improved, and by helping in native disputes weighed things in their own favour and obtained a footing for more help from their own lands. Some natives even received these into pay as auxiliary troops, and when fratricidal strife so weakened the natives, the foreigners took over.

Then the Danes, with a considerable fleet, in the hope of plunder made a descent on the island and plundered Dublin and the adjacent country. This alarmed the Norwegians who feared to be driven out, so they offered them battle and the Danes accepted and left a thousand Norwegians dead at Linn Duachaill in a complete victory.

They continued to plunder and to enlarge the territory taken over to plant settlements. Amhlaoibh, son of the king of Denmark, led them and they beat the natives in several fights and imposed heavy contributions on them and reduced them to a state of servitude.

About this time Olchabhair king of Munster died, as did Flaithnia the pious bishop of Biorra, and Cormac, the devout prelate of Lathraigh Broin.

Maolseachlann convoked the convention of Rath Aodha Mac Bric where the untiring diligence and importunity of Eatgna, who was a convert of Saint Patrick and who had entered into some religious order and was a saint of excellent holiness and devotion succeeded in getting agreement with Maolguala, king of Munster and Carrol. It was agreed that Maolguala, son of Dungaile and king of Munster, and Carrol, king of Ossery, should conclude a peace with Leath Cuinn, and that Carrol should submit to Eatgna.

Some time after this the Normans, in desperate fury, slew Maolguala with stones.

Maolseachlann engaged the Danes and slew great numbers of them and their troops at the Battle of Drum Da Moigh. Domhnal mac Ailpin, king of the Picts, died soon after this.

In AD 897 Maolseachlann died a natural death and was succeeded by Aodh Finnlaith, son of Niall Caille. His mother was Gormfhlaith daughter of Dinnis, son of Domhnal. His wife was Maolmuire, daughter of Cionaoith mac Ailpin, king of Scotland. Their son was Niall of Glendoo.

In this Aodh's reign, Connor son of Donoch, king of half Meath, was slain by Amhlaoibh, son of the son of the king of Denmark at Cluain Ioraid, who then transported a big number of Danes into Scotland where he slew many Picts and took many as slaves.

Aodh killed twelve hundred Lochlannaigh at Lough Foyle, among them forty principal commanders, and the Irish attacked the fortifications and garrisons of the invaders and got back the plunder and booty. Conall, bishop of Cill Sgire, died. Amhlaoibh's palace at Cluain Dalcain was burned to the ground causing great confusion. It was secretly set on fire by Gaoithin and Mac Ciaran the son of Roannan, and the Irish, taking advantage, slew one hundred of their principal commanders. Amhlaoibh, in revenge, ambushed and killed, wounded or took prisoner two thousand. He then went and plundered Armagh and the adjacent country in a furious rage and carried off valuables and paid his soldiers with them.

Cionfhaola son of Machtighern, thirteen years king of Munster, died, and Donnoch mac Dubhdabhiorionn seized the crown and proclaimed himself king.

The Danes slew great numbers of the Picts, and Roger son of Moirmin king of Wales fled to Ireland and was honourably received. The relics of Saint Colmcill were brought to Ireland for safety.

Lorcan mac Lachtna got the kingship of Thomond.

The pious Tighearnach, son of Muireadhaidh, bishop of Drum Ionasglan and Aodh Fionnlaith both died at Drum Ionasglan about the same time.

In AD 913 Flan Sionna, son of Maolseachlann, Maolruadhna (Eiremhom's line) succeeded. His mother was Lan, daughter of Dungoil, son of Feargoil, king of Ossery.

He soon invaded Munster, cruelly plundered and carried many into a wretched captivity. In his reign Domhnal son of Muireagein was treacherously slain by his own followers; Fiachna son of Ainbroith, son of Aodh Roin, king of Ulster one year, died, as did Donoch mac Dubhdabhlorionn of Munster.

The Danes, somewhat as robbers, plundered Cluain Ioraird and Kildare. Maolguala died at the Fair of Tailtean as it ended. He was king of Munster seven years.

The Normans, who had some part of Ireland, fell to Sitric Mac Iobhair and killed him. Aidhet, king of Ulster, was inhumanly murdered by his own subjects of Ulster, and the Danes of Loch Feabhail took advantage of the confusion to plunder Armagh. They surprised and captured Cumasgach, king of Ulster and his son Aodh.

Domhnal, son of Constantine king of Scotland, died.

The Danes feared the peace, unity, temporal and religious recovery of the Irish during the seven years that the holy king of Cashel Mhumhan, Cormac mac Cuillenan held the throne of Munster, for he was a peacemaker among the Gaels and a unifying force. They became afraid to plunder, and a great number went to their ships and left.

In a tragic invasion of Leinster into which Cormac was steered against his will King Flan helped Leinster, and Munster lost six thousand in the Battle of Beallach Mughna in a total defeat. King Cormac fell twice when on horseback and broke his neck and his back. His head was brought to Flan who, restraining his tears, took it in his hands and kissed it, lamenting the instability of greatness and the untimely death of so religious a prince and so venerable a prelate. Instead of a gratuity he upbraided those who brought it for their inhumanity and for violating the Law of Nations (Jus Gentium) which forbids the stabbing and mangling of the dead, and he chased them as barbarous ruffians who had no more veneration for the dignity and majesty of a king than for a common enemy. He gave strict orders for the body to be searched for and buried where his will or testament showed he wished to be buried. He made his will some days before the battle, knowing prophetically that his life would end soon.

(In his will he left an ounce of gold and silver, a horse and arms to Ard Fionnan (Drumabhradh), a golden and a silver chalice with a silk vestment to Liosmor, two similar chalices with four ounces of gold and five of silver to Cashel, three ounces of gold and a mass book to Imleach Iubhair, an ounce of gold and an ounce of silver to Glendaloch, a horse, arms, ounce of gold to Kildare with a silk vestment, twenty-four ounces of gold and silver to Armagh, et cetera.)

Flan seems to have died naturally, and was succeeded after a reign of thirty-eight years by Niall of Glendubh, often called Glundubh, son of Aodh Fionnlaith, son of Niall Caille. His mother was Maolmuire, daughter of Cionaoith mac Ailpin, king of Scotland.

Niall re-established the Fair of Tailtean. He slew a great umber of Lochlannaigh at Loch da Chaoch in a Pyrrhic victory.

In his reign the people of Leinster were totally routed by the Danes under Iomhair at Ceannfuaid where six hundred were killed, among them Mac Muireagonn, king of East Liffey, Ughaire, son of Oiliolla, Mogroin, son of Kennedy, king of Comanns and Leix, and also many generals.

Oittir, an able general of the Danes, transported choice troops from Loch da Chaoch into Scotland where Cuas son of Aodh fell upon them with such fury that he slaughtered many of them and the remainder fled to their ships without their general.

The Lochlannaigh under Sitric and the sons of Iomhair landed many men and they proceeded to plunder as usual and took Dublin with the sword. King Niall in haste collected the forces of Leath Cuinn but was defeated and slain at the Battle of Kilmashogue (south of Dublin), where the victors gave no quarter.

With him fell Connor mac Maolseachlain, prince of Ireland, Aodh mac Eochagain, king of Ulster, Maolmithigh son of

Flanagan, king of Breagh and Maolcraoibhe Ri Oirghial with many other brave men who sacrificed their lives for their people, their faith and their fatherland. King Niall was succeeded by Donoch after a three year reign. King Niall was buried on Tibradden, South Dublin and the remains of his grave are there still.

In AD 954 Donoch son of Flan Sionna of Eiremhon's line. His mother was Gormfhlaith, daughter of Flann, son of Conuing. He reigned thirty years.

In his time Ceallachan son of Buadhachan was king of both provinces of Munster for ten years. Before he became king, when the throne became vacant, Kennedy son of Lorcan came to Gleanamhuin (north Co. Cork) with a numerous retinue to treat with the nobles about his becoming king of Munster, but Ceallachan's mother intervened and pointed out that it was not his turn to rule according to the will of Oilioll Olum – that right being with her son, and she requested him not to violate the ancient legislation. Kennedy stepped down, letting right have precedence over might.

The Danes disturbed his reign, but when their violence did not succeed and lacked hope of success they tried treachery.

Sitric, son of Turgil, having taken counsel, sent to Ceallachan notifying him that he intended for them to have peace and a good understanding, that he would withdraw his forces and hostilities, make no future attempt on the crown of Munster, and make a league for the defence of both parties, that he would give hostages and give his sister to him in marriage, and aid him in offensive war and would expect him to do likewise.

As this princess was well known by all to be beautiful and virtuous, Ceallachan was delighted to accept, and at Kennedy's advice did not take most of the Munster forces with him to bring her with great honour to Cashel – only some of his bodyguard. As soon as possible he set out for Dublin, leaving Kennedy the Prince of Munster in charge; he who had stepped down most honourably.

Morling, Sitric's wife, who was a daughter of Aodh mac Eochaidh (Keogh now) expostulated with Sitric who was going to kill Ceallachan for such treachery and she made her plan to save him.

Sitric had told Donoch the Ard-ri of his intention, and he approved and promised friendship after the event would take place – Munster had refused to pay its contributions and chief rents.

Rising early, Morling came out of Dublin by the way Ceallachan would come and told him of the plot; that he was to be killed after the wedding – she had left Sitric under the impression that she approved.

He was greatly surprised and thanked her, and, taking her leave, headed back for Munster, but Sitric had lined the hedges with armed Danes and laid so many ambushes for him that it was impossible for him to escape.

In a desperate conflict many Munster principal men were slain as were also Danes, but fresh help came from Dublin and after a fierce fight they got the upper hand and took Ceallachan and Duncuan son of Kennedy prisoners, but only after a long and resolute resistance. They stripped and plundered the dead.

Nine Danish noblemen were appointed to take them to Armagh and they were given a strong force to guard the prisoners, who were kept with great strictness and severity. The survivors, when they reached Munster, reported the treachery of the Danes. The whole province was alarmed and Kennedy was determined on a rescue. Veterans and fresh troops were ready… a formidable army and also a fleet of ships well fitted out and well manned.

Donoch Mac Keeffe commanded the army and Kennedy reminded him of his noble blood and the magnanimity of his ancestors – kings of Munster – whom he named with honour and due applause mentioning their exploits and how they had exposed their lives to danger for the good of their country and had repelled the insolent invaders who were foreign to Ireland. He said that under his command the prospects of success were very good indeed, and that under his conduct and bravery he was certain the Danes would be chastised for violating the law of nations and the established rights of hospitality.

Kennedy ordered a thousand brave Dalgais under his brothers Cosgrach, Lonergan and Conghallach to go with the expedition, and he raised five hundred more of the Dal gCais whom he gave into the command of Sioda of the Clan Cuillean and five hundred more of the same tribe under the command of Deaghadh son of Domhnal who also commanded the volunteers from the nobility of Munster and Thomond (North Munster).

Failbhe Fionn commanded the fleet and it sailed to the left. The land army went through Connacht where they halted and sent out parties to forage and to get provisions from Ierne and Umhall, but these they abandoned when the scouts reported that an army was marching towards them.

The main body was immediately put on the alert, but were delighted to find they were more Munster people coming to join them. They were from the Gaileangaidh and the Luighnidh. Their captain said most of them were the posterity of Cian, the great son of Oilioll Ollum. The rest were men of Dealbhna descended from the renowned Dealbhaoith, son of Cas son of Conal Eachluath; that they were resolved to risk their lives against those barbarous Danes who, by basest treachery, kept their king in unjust captivity. He had three officers of signal courage: Aodh son of Dualgaia, over the Gaileangaidh, Diarmuid mac Fianachtaigh, over the Luighnidh, and Dinis Mac Maoldomhnaigh, over the Dealbhna.

This new and unexpected force had five hundred expert archers and five hundred with swords and shields.

This army plundered the adjacent country and destroyed a number of inhabitants. Mortoch son of Arnalaig applied to Donoch mac Keeffe for the return of the booty insisting that it was unjust to oppress those not concerned in hostilities who rather should be protected, but Donoch only agreed to return what was over when the army was fed.

Mortoch was angry and sent a secret message to inform the Danes in Armagh. The nine Earls, sons of Turgil, were very alarmed at this news and drew out most of their troops out of Armagh to meet Munster, who soon learned that the prisoners were taken to Sitric's ship. Donoch mac Keeffe gave no quarter to the Danish force and the next morning marched to Dundalk and found all the Danes had taken to their ships with their prisoners.

Angry frustration boiled in the Munster land army, but they soon saw a fleet on the sea coming briskly with the wind – it was their own. It drew up in line of battle, and surprised the Danes.

Failbhe Fionn fell upon the ship where Sitric and his brothers Tor and Magnus were and with irresistible force boarded her. When he saw Ceallachan tied to the mast a flood of fresh courage made his fury more irresistible as he laid about him and, having slain several Danes, he cut Ceallachan's cords, put a sword in his hand and said to him to take charge of the ship he had left without a commander and leave him to deal with Sitric.

This was done and Failbhe Fionn fought well till overcome by numbers and loss of blood that weakened him. He was slain, hacked and mangled, and at last beheaded.

Sitric's skill and bravery together with his brother's Tor and that of Magnus and that of his bodyguard made victory for the Irish more than doubtful for some time.

Fiongall followed Failbhe Fionn on board the Dane, and maintained his post slaying Danes till the deck ran with blood, but Danish numbers being superior he found himself unable to hold ground any longer so, seizing upon Sitric by the collar, he grasped him close and threw himself, with Sitric in his arms, into the sea where both perished.

Seaghdha (shay) and Conal, two captains seeing this, fell to the Danes with dreadful fury, cut their way to Tor and Magnus, Sitric's brothers, rushed violently on them, seized them both in their arms and jumped with them overboard, where all drowned.

At this the great courage of the Danes began to abate and Munster seeing this took advantage with such success that they boarded most of the Danish ships, killing and destroying till completely victorious – though many brave officers and soldiers were mourned by widows and orphans of Munster after this terrible sea fight that historians describe as the most dreadful and terrible of any that happened upon these coasts for many ages. The officers and men did outstanding work on both sides – dominion and liberty being the prize.

The Munster land army were distracted as they watched the fight; they ran up and down the coast in fury but were unable to join in the fight to help their brave brothers, but were somewhat consoled at the way the Munster fleet was succeeding in destroying the Danish fleet – all but some that escaped by flight and were not overtaken.

When the work was done the land-army received their brothers with open arms and joyful victorious cheers. They were overjoyed to see their king again and that he was safe; he was no less overjoyed at his deliverance and safety from the death that continually hung over him, and he retained great gratitude for his sea and land forces.

He praised highly his sea forces for their bravery, ordered supplies for them and gave instructions for the care of the wounded and marched back to Munster. On his way Mortoch mac Flann king of Leinster was determined to hinder his march, but desisted through fear of what the victorious Munster men would do to him for siding with the enemy of Ireland.

Ceallachan and his army were ripe for clearing out the Danes and when he got things ready he attacked Limerick, killed five hundred and took the rest prisoners. He found five hundred of the Danish army in the Cashel district and put them to the sword. Another Sitric, a general, tried to recover the booty but had to retire, leaving five hundred more dead, and just escaped himself by fleeing to his shipping.

Ceallachan married a daughter of Domhnal O'Faolan, king of the Deisies, whose name was Gormfhlat and who was of great beauty and of exemplary virtue, but not very long after he died in peace, and was succeeded by Feargna, son of Ailgeanan son of Dungala; but he was treacherously murdered by a set of conspirators, near relatives of his own.

The crown of Munster was then seized by Mahon son of Kennedy, his brother Eichiarun being over Thomond.

Mahon's brother Brian had the principal command of the Munster army when Mahon fell upon the Danes at the Battle of Sulchoid, wherein two thousand of the Danish army were slain with Teitill, strong champion governor of Waterford, Ruanon governor of Cork, Muiris the governor of Limerick, Bernard and Toroil, two first rank officers, together with those slain on the streets and in the houses of Limerick where the victorious army pursued the fleeing Danes giving neither mercy nor quarter.

Mahon bestowed the plunder of the city on the soldiers – an immense booty of jewels, gold, silver and rich furniture. He left the town incapable of defence, having demolished the walls and burned the fortifications and houses.

After this victory Mahon was betrayed, seized in his own palace, conducted as a prisoner under strong guard to Mac Broin where he was barbarously put to death by the people of that place though Saint Colum mac Ciaragain tried to get his life saved.

In the reign of this king Donoch the pious bishop of Tuileim died; and about that time Donoch invaded Connacht but lost heavily at Dubhthir near Athlone where Cionaoth, son of Connor king of Faile, was slain. Soon after this the Danes plundered Cluain mac Nois, went to Loch Ribh and dreadfully ravaged both sides of the adjoining country, spoiled Ein Inis, and, after a sharp engagement twelve hundred Irish were slain.

Within a short time twelve hundred Danes perished at Loch Rughruidh.

By a strategy of the Danes of Dublin they succeeded in capturing Faolan king of Leinster and his children. Dun Sobhairce was spoiled by the Danes of Loch Cuain, and Kildare by the Danes of Waterford. The province of Ulster rose against them with fury and left eight hundred foreigners dead with three commanders: Albdan, Aufear and Roilt. Mortoch Mac Neill was the Irish general.

The effects of this were felt through the kingdom. The Danes were dispirited and there was tranquillity until, encouraged by their countrymen, they made an attack on the Fair of Roscrea under Olfinn, but the Irish, knowing their treachery, brought their arms and, when they heard they were coming, left everything. Their unanimity, courage and charge left four thousand dead and Olfinn, their leader.

About this time Tadhg son of Cathall, twenty years king of Connacht, died, as did Sitric mac Iomhair king of the Danes and Norwegians in Ireland.

The Connacht people defeated them around Loch Oirbhsionn (Corrib). Conuing mac Neill slew twelve hundred of them at Loch Neachach (na nEochaidheacht) but they went to Loch Eirne and did frightful destruction. Godfrey, commander of Loch Cuain, invaded and harassed the province of Armagh, spoiling and rifling churches. Ambrose his son spoiled Cilcuillen, destroyed the country, and took a thousand prisoners.

Greenan Ely in Donegal was plundered and Mortoch mac Neill captured but he freed himself by a stratagem.

Connacht killed Arolt mac Iomhair, governor of Limerick under the Danes.

About this time Ambrose mac Godfrey, king of the Lochlannaigh in Ireland, was slain by the Normans who landed and attempted a conquest of Ireland.

Roderick, a prince of Wales, landed a Welsh army to plunder, spoil and take possession of Ireland, but he lost his life and most of his army was destroyed. Congallach son of Maolmithigh took Dublin from the Danes and plundered it in AD 966 and seven hundred and forty were slain.

Donoch the king died naturally and was succeeded by Congall son of Maolmithigh, Flanagan, Ceallach, Conuing, Congalla and Aodh Slaine, of Eiremhon's race. His mother was Mary, daughter of Cionaoth mac Ailpin.

In his reign Eitimont king of England and Blathchuire king of Normandy died.

The Lochlannaigh became very active, but in the Pyrrhic victory of Muine Breogain he killed seven thousand.

In his fourth year reigning, Brian son of Kennedy became king of the two provinces of Munster, and inside two years sent one of his heralds at arms to challenge Meills mac Broin king of Oneachach to a pitched battle on plains of Beallach Leachta because of Mahon's murder. (We read in 'Saint Patrick after the ancient narrations': 'Derbhall opposed him and said, "If you can remove the mountain there before us so that I can see Loch Lungha over it to the south in the Plain of Fir Maighe Feine I will believe." Ceannfebhret is the name of the mountain which immediately began to melt, and Beallach Leachta – the pass of melting is the name of the pass that then opened.)'

Meills (Maol Muaidh) accepted the challenge and enlisted the help of fifteen hundred Lochlannaigh but Brian with the Dal gCais broke through all opposition with terrible slaughter and a general rout. The Danes fled but were pursued and great numbers were slain and the rest taken prisoners.

Domhnal O'Faolan king of the Deisies was not pleased at Brian for this and with the support of a formidable body of Danes invaded Munster with the cruelty of an enraged enemy. Brian overtook them when they were plundering Fan Conrach. He so terrorised the Danes that they were routed and Domhnal had to fly for his life. Brian chased Danes and Domhnal's men into Waterford, put all to the sword, sacked the town and burned it. Domhnal lost his life.

Brian when about eight years reigning, imposed tribute on all Leath Modha, but after Domhnal Claon died, his son, the Leinster people and the Danes refused the tribute, so Brian invaded and fought the Battle of Glenmama and left five thousand Danes and Irish dead.

Brian was a scourge for the Danes having routed them in twenty-five battles.

After Glenmama, Congall son of Maolmithigh invaded Munster and put Eichiaruin and Dunchuan, sons of Kennedy, to the sword.

Godfrey mac Sitric and his Lochlannaigh spoiled Ceananus, Domhnach-Padraig, Ard Breaccan, Cill Sgirre and other sacred places.

They took off with them three thousand prisoners, gold, silver and other things of great value.

About this time Eithne daughter of Feargoll, who had been queen of Ireland, died. Also Maolcullum mac Domhnal, king of Scotland, and Gaoithne the most religious bishop of Dun Da Leathglass and also Teighe mac Cathill, king of Connacht.

In AD 994 Congall the Ard-ri fell into the hands of the Danes who served in the provincial army of Leinster and they killed him at Armagh. He was succeeded after a reign of ten years by Domhnal son of Mortoch son of Niall of Glendoo. In his reign Amhlaoimh mac Sitric with the Dublin Danes plundered the country of Kildare. Domhnal plundered Connacht under provocation and took much booty and many prisoners – Feargal O'Rourke being too weak to oppose him. The great Church of Tuam was built by Cormac O'Cilline, the pious bishop of Tuam Greine. Feargal O'Rourke was killed by Domhnal son of Congall son of Maolmithigh. Brian son of Kennedy assaulted the Danes of Limerick and burned the city. Domhnal O'Neill plundered Leinster from the Barrow east to the sea and Danes and Leinster men were not able to dislodge him; he remained two months there (he was king of Ulster).

Near this time Maolfinnin, son of Uchtan, the pious bishop of Ceananus (Kells) and venerable confessor of Ultan died. The Danes, under the command of Amhlaoimh Cuarain, supported by the army of Leinster (which was under their own general), plundered Ceananus, took much spoil, impoverished the people thereby and reduced them to misery.

Domhnal son of Congall, helped by the Dublin Danes, fought the Battle of Cillmona against Domhnal son of Mortoch king of Ireland, with great slaughter on both sides. Ardgall, king of Ulster for seventeen years, son of Madagan and Donnagan mac Maolmuire king of Oirghiallach with many others were slain.

The most religious Beacan, bishop of Finne, died soon after this time.

Cionaoth O'Hartigan Primate of Armagh assisted the Lochlannaigh of Dublin to capture Ughaire son of Tuathal, king of Leinster.

Brian son of Kennedy killed eight hundred Danes of Inis Catha and made prisoners of Iomhair, Amhlaoimh and Dubhgeann their chiefs.

The Dublin Danes fought the provincial troops of Leinster and beat them, and in the Battle of Boithlione, Ugaire the king of Leinster was slain.

In AD 1004 after a reign of ten years Domhnal died naturally at Armagh and was succeeded by Maolseachluin the second, son of Domhnall, son of Donough, son of Flann Sionna (of Eiremhon's line). His mother was Dunflath the daughter of Mortoch mac Neill who was also the mother of the king of the Danes in Ireland; Glunioruin.

In his reign five thousand Lochlannaigh were slain by him at the Battle of Tara. They were chiefly Danes of Dublin and the sons of Amhlaoimh. Randle, son of Amlaoimh was king of the Danes in Ireland and was among the slain.

Maolseachluin joined forces with Eochaidh son of Ardgail (thirty-five years king of Ulster) and they attacked Dublin to drive the foreigners out of Ireland. They attacked most violently after three days' siege, slaughtered many and fixed their standard on the walls and the Danes were terrified and surrendered and were treated with humanity and moderation. Many Irish prisoners were released – gentry who had suffered long and severe confinement. The hostages of O'Neill and Donal Claon king of Leinster were freed. The terms were to relinquish all their conquests from the Shannon to the Irish Sea, to forbear all hostilities, and to give whatever tribute would be imposed. Amhlaoimh was banished and fled to Iona.

Maolseachluin quarrelled with the Dal gCais and burned Bile Moigh Adair, but Brian revenged this.

The three sons of Carrol, son of Lorcan took and plundered Glen Da Loch but were found dead the night afterwards. Saint Caomhgin had consecrated that place for divine worship and use.

About this time Morling, daughter of Cealla, died, and also Ioraid Mac Coisie primate of Armagh. (Morling was the queen.)

The Danes prepared for new attempts and under Mortoch O'Congallach plundered Domhach Padric with great cruelty, but were soon chastised by an epidemic that took great numbers of them. Maolseachluin fought them with success and took and wore the collar of gold one of their champions had worn, having foiled him in a hand-to-hand fight – his name was Tomar. He fought Carolus a chief commander and having foiled him, took his sword.

The Danes gradually gained in strength, got new forces from abroad and were not opposed vigorously by Maolseachluin, but Brian son of Kennedy hunted and harassed them successfully and vigorously so that Munster and Connacht began to look to him as a true saviour and to desire for him to take on the defence of all Ireland by becoming Ard-ri. They asked Brian and it was unanimously agreed to ask Maolseachluin to resign because of incompetence and lack of vigour in defence of Ireland and for letting the Danes go unpunished, and to ask him to step down in favour of a man who would stand up to them and let Ireland enjoy peace.

The messengers pointed out the advantages that his peaceful resignation would be to the Irish and the advantages that the Irish were sure to get under the protection of so vigorous, powerful and meritorious a person as Brian, and that the nobility and gentry were determined to dethrone him.

He refused with scorn and indignation to comply or to meet the Munster nobility as they requested at Magh Da Chaomhog, stating his determination to maintain his position to the last.

Brian, hearing this, made up his mind to seize the crown, and helped by paid Danes he marched towards Tara but sent a herald to summon Maolseachluin to resign and send hostages or, if he refused, to let the sword decide. Maolseachluin was unprepared and asked Brian for a month to find what help he could get together. Brian agreed and kept his army in camp peaceably till further orders.

Maolseachluin convened the principal nobility of Leath Cuinn and he despatched messengers. He sent his antiquary to the Great O'Neill, to Eochaidh son of Ardgail king of Ulster and to Cathal O'Connor king of Connacht for immediate aid or to send their hostages to Brian – for those were his terms.

Hugh O'Neill said his ancestors defended Tara when they had it, and if he was not able to keep it to let it go to Brian, and that he esteemed Brian's friendship.

Hearing this, and fearing the effects of this on the others, Maolseachluin sent to him and offered him Tara with undisputed succession for his descendants, but Hugh hesitated, and he called a meeting of the Siol Eoghain to get their views. They inclined to not trust Maolseachluin but advised Hugh to give him a civil answer while refusing help. They met again and, knowing they would lose their lives if they fought the invincible Dal gCais who never turned back, they resolved to venture if they got conditions equal to the hazard: one half of the country of Meath and the lands of Tara so as to provide for their wives and children if and when they were defeated. Maolseachluin looked on these as exorbitant and unjust and went home. He summoned Clan Colman, stated the case, and was counselled to submit.

He took twelve hundred horses and was admitted to Brian's presence and was received with great courtesy. He told Brian how his circumstances were, that it was not through cowardice he submitted, for he was determined to fight, but was not able.

Brian understood how he felt, offered him a year to repair his broken fortune, said he would take no hostages but would rely on his honour to fulfil the terms at the end of the year. In the meantime he would visit Hugh and Eochaidh to test their attitude and told Maolseachluin he could join on their side if at that time it came to blows. But Maolseachluin assured him he would not do any such thing and advised Brian not to go north at this time – which advice then suited Brian's larder, for provisions were low. Brian gave Maolseachluin two hundred and forty fine horses and gave his retinue very magnificent gifts of gold and silver, and both kings parted with mutual respect.

At the end of the year Brian mustered vigorously, summoned Irish and Danes to enter his service, and there came the Irish and Danes of Waterford, Wexford, Oneachach, Corcoluigheach and Ui Cinnsalach. He marched to Athlone, received hostages from Connacht and Maolseachluin sent his.

He marched towards Dundealgan where he overcame some opposition and got the submission of the rest of Ireland.

He became Ard-ri and set about governing in a wise efficient and peace-promoting way, so that by gifts, pardons and privileges he won the greater part of Ireland over to him, and they became his loyal subjects and things began to go well and people began to breath the air of security and live in peace and harmony under the reign of Brian.

Brian Boru was king for twelve years, Brian son of Kennedy, Lorcan, Lachtna, Cathal, Corc, Anluan, Mahon, Turlach, Cathal, Aodh Caomh, Conall, Eochaidh Baldearg, Carthan Fionn, Blod, Cas, Conal Eachluath, Luighdheach Meann, Aongus, Fearchorb, Modhchorb, Cormac Cas and Oilioll Ollum, of the Heber Fionn line. His mother was Beibhionn Cianog daughter of Archadh, king of west Connacht.

In Brian's reign, Sitric son of Amlaoimh fitted out a fleet, plundered the coasts of Ulster with great cruelty, ransacked and destroyed Cill Cleithe and Inis Comeasgraidh, taking valuables and many prisoners. The pious Naomhan son of Maolciaran, primate of Ireland died and also Randle, son of Goffa, king of the Isle of the Danes.

Brian, with a strong force, marched to Cinel Eoghain in Ulster, then to Meath, staying for a week. He laid twenty ounces of gold on the alter of Armagh. He went to Dalnaruide and received the Ulster hostages. He went soon to Tir Conaill and was acknowledged lawful king of Ireland.

Maolruana son of Ardgail king of Ulster died, also the learned Clothna, son of Aongus, principal poet; and Cathall O'Connor, twenty years king of Connacht, died at Inis Domhnain.

Mortoch son of Brian with troops of Munster and Leinster, assisted by Flathbheartach son of Muireadhach (Cinal Eoghain) plundered the Cinel Luigheach (around Killmacrennan) taking great spoils and three hundred prisoners. Brian surprised Maolruadhna O'Doraidh king of the Cinel Conaill at Magh Coruinn and took him to Ceann Coradh as a prisoner.

Mortoch son of Brian raged through Leinster with fire and sword as far as Glen Da Loch and then he came to Kilmainham. The Danes put to sea and landed on the coast of Munster, committed dreadful ravages, plundered and burned Cork but soon after this Amhlaoimh son of Sitric king of the Danes and Mathghamhuin son of Dubhgoil were seized and killed by Dubhdabhoireann. About this time the Leinster people together with the Danes of Leinster entered Meath and plundered Tarmuin Feicin with great cruelty and took a multitude of prisoners, but the hand of God was seen in punishment, for they perished soon after by exemplary inflictions from heaven.

Brian, as soon as he got established in peace, began to carry out repairs to a disordered Ireland. He bestowed gifts, showed clemency and generosity, and made a general peace and security prevail; and all were grateful for this.

He convened the clergy, found out their rights and restored them and recovered the revenues of the Church seized by the Danes who used them for purposes never intended by the donors, who made the sacrifice of those to the Lord.

When he had put religion back into its honoured position he next arranged for the education of youth. He repaired the public schools, destroyed by the foreign enemies of learning, erected new academies where needed, built public libraries for poor students and made provision for brilliant students in all professions.

He enriched universities and they were governed by regular discipline with the effect that persons of excellent ability revived the decayed state of learning so that Irish youth taught and refined neighbouring nations. He helped farmers and restored to the owners who were still alive the property taken by the Lochlannaigh. No nepotism was known in his court nor favouritism, and no 'legal' robbery nor oppression of anybody.

He appointed surnames to be taken in order that families could be distinguished and to facilitate the proper keeping of genealogies and facilitate taxation (some families took a saint's name and put the prefix Giolla, servant, or Maol-tonsured, in honour of, before it, others took O or Ui, descendant (or grandson) of a remote ancestor, others took Mac, son of their own father). We also find a combination of some of those prefixes as Mac Giolla Bhrighid – son of the Servant of Saint Brigid.

Brain built the great church of Killaloo, of Inis Cealtrach, and he repaired the steeple of Tuam Greine. He laid causeways, built bridges, raised fortifications where needed and manned them. He fortified Cashel, Cean Feabhradh, Inis Locha Cea, Inis Loch Guir, Dun Eochair Maighe, Dun Iasc, Dun Trilliag, Dun gCrot, Dun Cliath, Inis an Gaill Dubh, Inis Loch Saighlean, Ros na Riogh and Ceann Coradh.

He purged, corrected and established laws and inspired his subjects with such respect for honour, integrity, justice, and virtue that a beautiful young lady undertook a journey from the north of Ireland adorned with jewels and a most costly dress to the Wave of Cliodna (daughter of Geannon) and no person tried to injure her nor to dishonour her nor to rob her of the ring she carried openly on a stick, nor of her rich cloak. She travelled on foot. This transaction is narrated in an old Gaelic poem, and a more modern Irish poet has narrated it in English. It starts: 'Rich and rare were the gems she wore.'

Peace brought prosperity and the twelve years of Brian's reign were a gift from God after the agonies of more than two hundred years.

Brian's tributes each year were specified by public law thus: eight hundred cows and eight hundred hogs from Connacht at 1st November; five hundred cloaks and five hundred cows from Tir Conaill; sixty hogs and sixty loads of iron from Tir Eoghain; one hundred and fifty cows and one hundred and fifty hogs from the Clanna Rughraide; one hundred and sixty cows from the

Oirgiallach; three hundred beeves and three hundred hogs and three hundred loads of iron from Leinster; sixty beeves, sixty hogs and sixty loads of iron from Ossery; one hundred and fifty hogsheads of wine from the Danes of Dublin; one hundred and fifty hogsheads of red wine from the Danes of Limerick.

Only the Dal gCais were permitted to have arms at court. Brian lived at Ceann Coradh leaving Maolseachluin at Tara.

He saw the necessity for having a fleet superior to what the Danes would have if they again struck – as they might do any time anywhere – so he asked his brother-in-law Maolmordha mac Murchuda to send him three of the longest and largest trees he could find to make masts. The king of Leinster at once complied and at Sliabh an Bhoguigh there arose a contest between which of the three tribes carrying them should go first. The king dismounted and he decided in favour of the Ui Faolan and put his shoulder under the burden like the rest, but the fastener of the cloak that Brian had presented him with flew off. It was the law that the Ard-ri should make definite presentations to the kings he visited, as for example he gave the king of Tir Conaill twenty steeds, twenty complete armours and twenty cloaks; for which this king supported him and the nobility of Munster for a month and then escorted him to Tir Eoghain. All were received with friendly courtesy and suitably rewarded.

Maolmordha asked his sister Brian's wife to repair the cloak but she pulled the cloak from his shoulders and threw it into the fire, giving out to him at the same time that he had let down the honour of their noble family and his posterity. He kept things quiet, made no fuss. The next day Morroch son of Brian was playing chess with Conuing son of Dunchuain, and Maolmordha looking on gave advice that caused Conuing to win. Morroch resented this and was angry and told Maolmordha that it was by his advice that the Danes lost the Battle of Glenmama (Madhma). 'If that was so the next time I advise them they'll retrieve the loss.' 'Make sure there is a yew tree near,' said Morroch (he had been found hiding in a yew tree after the rout). 'And the Danes have been chastised so often by us that even if the king of Leinster was at their head we would have no reason to fear.'

Maolmordha retired to his quarters, refused to eat, burned

with indignant resentment, refused to drink publicly and, rising early next morning, left in a secret way, determined on revenge.

Brian sent Cogaran after him with the message that he was to return to receive the gifts which he had ready as a token of thanks. But, having delivered the message, he had to be carried on a stretcher across the Shannon again to Kincora with a skull broken by three hard blows of Maolmordha's walking stick.

Brian restrained his troops who wanted to pursue for they considered that as Cogaran was the king's messenger it was not in his Majesty's honour to permit an indignity like this to be overlooked. But Brian knew that Maolmordha had received an affront in his palace against the laws of hospitality and told them he would chastise him at his own door.

Maolmordha immediately summoned the principal nobility, told them the indignity he had suffered and in such a way that the whole assembly immediately decided to join the power of the Lochlannaigh against the king of Ireland and fight him.

Brian had expelled the Lochlannaigh from Ireland except from Dublin, Wexford, Waterford, Cork and Limerick for these were useful for trade, supplies and tribute.

At Maolmordha's request the king of Denmark sent twelve thousand men to Dublin under Carl Cnut and Andrew, his two sons; Broder was general. Many other contingents of Danes arrived in Dublin Bay... from Norway, Sweden, Orkney Islands, Shetland, Skye, Lewis, Cantire, Caithness, Hebrides and the Isle of Man.

Maolmordha sent a challenge to Brian (who had heard of the arrival of the Danes) to fight him at Clontarf. Brian accepted. There was consternation in Ireland and grave anticipation of what the results would or might be – would fighting and turmoil start again and the Danes have a hand in it?

But Brian the brave mustered his Munster forces and the brave men of Connacht came in droves to help him. Maolseachluin also came.

Great patriotism animated Brian's army and they had great hope of a meritorious victory, and Ireland knew Brian's ability and what his invincible Dalcassians would and could do.

When Brian reached Dublin he sent choice troops under his

son Donoch to raid Leinster and to return in two days. These consisted of Dal gCais and Eoghanacht. This was reported to Maolmordha by a messenger from Maolseachluin who urged him to attack the next day when these were away, promising him that he would pull off his troops at the beginning of the battle – which he did. But towards the end of the battle he joined in on Brian's side with the effect that fresh troops can have at such a time.

The forces opposing Brian had prepared during the night for an early attack and took up positions; Maolmordha in the centre with his Leinster forces, except the patriotic O'Moores and O'Nolans. The forces from Leinster numbered nine thousand.

On his left the Danes of Dublin under their king Sitric and the princes Dulat and Conmaol with a thousand mail-clad infantry from Norway under Carlus and Anrud sons of Uric king of Norway. On the right were the foreigners from the Baltic districts and from the Scottish Islands with aid from Wales and Cornwall. They were commanded by Sigurd, Earl of Orkneys and by Brodar, Admiral of the fleet.

Brian also arranged in three divisions. On the side next Dublin under Morroch were Tigue, Domhnal, Connor and Flan, brothers of Morroch and the brave Dalcassians, and Maolseachluin's thousand men. Beyond these were the forces of South Munster under Cian son of Maolmhuaidh (Molloy) and Domhnal son of Dubhdabhoran both of the Eoghanacht, Mothla son of Faolan king of the Decies, Muircheartach chief of Ui Liathain, Scannlan chief of Loch Lein, Loingseach (Lynch) king of Ui Conail Gabhra son of Dunlaing, Cathal son of Donobhan chief of Cairbre-Eva, Mac Beatha chief of Ciarraidhe Luachra, Geibhionnach son of Dubhgan chief of Fear Muighe, O'Carrol king of Eile, O'Carrol king of Oriel, and Maguire of Fear Manach.

Farther out in the Dollymount direction were the brave men of Connact under Taighg O'Kelly chief of Ui Maine, O'hAidhne chief of Ui Fiachra Aidhne, Dunlaing O'hArtagan, Eichiaran king of Dal Aradia and others.

A Dane, a big warrior, came out and thundered a challenge to any man in the Irish ranks to fight him single-handed. He was told that Domhnal (mac Eimhin, mac Cainig) accepted his challenge. He was the Maor Mor of Marr who came with Lennox of the Scottish Gaels, to help Brian. The Dane when ready again thundered along the lines: 'Where is Domhnal?' 'Reptile, I'm here.' Plat the Dane was dead first.

Brian rode along the Irish lines with a Crucifix in one hand and a sword in the other and exhorted his men in suitable words pointing out to them that on Good Friday, the Lord had died (that day was Good Friday), that these foes had desecrated all the holy churches, sacred vessels and sacred persons and holy relics, that they would repeat their sacrilegious crimes unless defeated that day, that the Lord had given them the opportunity and the strength to free the Irish from such oppression, looked down with pity on the sufferings and given the courage to destroy the foe and that He would be with them to requite the sacrilegious tyrants with the sword.

'Attack now, sword in hand.'

There was courage on both sides; no giving of ground. Commanders and chiefs met in single combat and destroyed each other, the intense action lasted about eight hours, the fight about twelve.

When Maolmordha and his chiefs had fallen his division began to give ground. The Irish one-handed battle-axe did fearful execution. Morroch split Sitric son of Lodar to the rump with one blow. Twice he cut down the standard-bearer of the Lochlannaigh. Carlus and Anrud rushing at him together were both slain and lanes were opened by him in the lines of the Lochlannaigh. Not one of the mail-clad Norwegians escaped alive, and they were a thousand. There was neither time nor opportunity to take prisoners.

Maolseachluin pulled out at the start but helped Brian towards evening. Morroch went back at times to bathe his swollen arm in a place of water but the Danes seeing this filled up the hole. Morroch kept on fighting and, shaking Anrud out of his mail and dashing him to the ground, his right arm borrowed the weight of his body to press his weapon through the Norwegian prince on the ground, but the brave fighting Norwegian prince pulled out Morroch's knife and mortally wounded him and, after receiving the Sacrament of Penance and the Holy Viaticum, he died.

Four thousand of the Danes of Dublin were slain in the first charge; Leinster lost three thousand one hundred. The foreigners who even brought their wives to take up residence in Ireland when they had beaten Brian lost six thousand seven hundred. The Danes and foreigners lost nearly all their chiefs and principal men. 'All perished by the sword,' said a survivor when asked where his companions were, but many perished in water when making for their ships – it would not have been easy for a Gaelic historian to give exact numbers, and besides these, many foreign women perished; some, it is narrated by a foreign author, 'leaped into the water in despair,' but these and others might have tried to come on shore to help their husbands and sons who were trying to escape or whom they saw wounded and sorely needing help but were overcome by the tide and by their dread of the victors after what they knew they had done to the Irish.

Many widows and orphans were made on both sides in that long day of woe for the invaders who were put on the defensive from the start.

The Irish lost about four thousand slain and many wounded and our great king Brian himself was killed but the Irish people are still grateful and still in admiration at the great deliverance brought by the power of God and the courage and surpassing bravery of Brian and the Munster and Connacht, kings, chiefs and soldiers and all who gave a helping hand on the day of Ireland's need.

Our wounded were brought to Kilmainham and their wounds dressed. Brain had received the rites of the church. The Monks of Sord Colmcille came and took the bodies of Brian, Morroch, Toirdhealach and Conuing son of Dunchuan to Sord – then on to Saint Ciarain's of Duleek. The monks of Duleek took them to Louth and the Coarb of Saint Patrick with his clergy came and took them to Armagh where the obsequies lasted twelve days with masses, prayers and waking day and night for their souls, and then they buried Brian at the north side of the cathedral church, and Morroch, Toirdhealach (Turlough) and Conuing at the south side in another tomb.

We find this poem dealing with Brian:

> The most renowned Brian Boru
> was slain one thousand four and thirty years
> After the birth of Christ

and it continues:

> In the most dreadful fight of Clontarf
> Was slain the valiant monarch of the Island
> After a life of eighty and eight years.

A nearby spectator wrote:

> I never beheld with my eyes nor read in history an account of a sharper and bloodier fight than this memorable action; nor if an angel from heaven would descend and relate the circumstances of it could you without difficulty be induced to give credence to it.
> I withdrew with the troops under my command and was no way otherwise concerned than as a spectator and stood at no greater distance than the breadth of a fallow field and a ditch. When both powerful armies engaged and grappled in close fight it was dreadful to behold how the swords glittered over their heads being struck by the rays of the sun which gave them an appearance of a numerous flock of white seagulls flying in the air. The strokes were so mighty and the fury of the combatants so terrible that great quantities of hair torn or cut off their heads by the sharp weapons were driven far off by the wind, and their spears and battle-axes were so encumbered with hair cemented with blood that it was scarce possible to clear or to bring them to their former brightness'.
> The day after the battle, Holy Saturday, the boy Toirdhealach, son of Morroch, was found at the Weir of the Tolca with his hands in the hair of a dead invader.

We salute the noble highborn and comely Dalcassians.

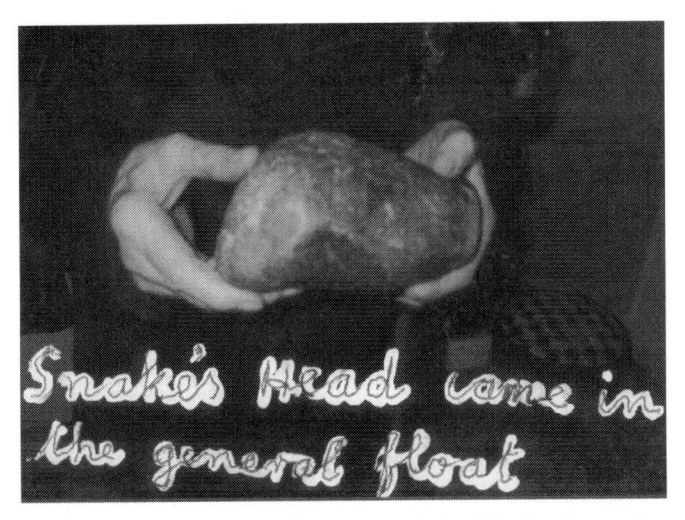

Snake's head carried in the general float. Part towards the tail also found, measuring about eight inches in length. (Greenhills).

Giant's Causeway, Co. Antrim. Of same period as the Sea of Deluge.

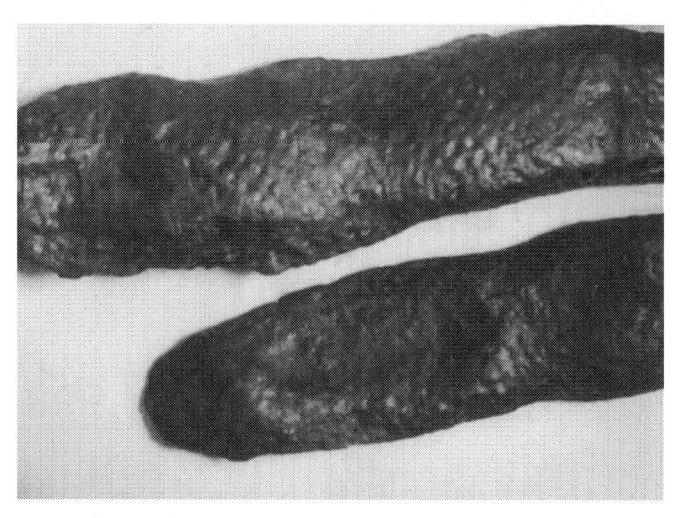

Found at Castlecomer coal mine. Broken in centre. Not yet identified, but indentation clearly visible.

Tidal layerings in southern Namibia and north-west South Africa. Tide going in one direction laid these down, and tide in the other direction made the divisions, as in Ireland. Two tides per day. Shows clearly the universal nature of the flood.

Large petrified tree on the surface of a petrified forest, Namibia. All of the surrounding rocks are petrified timber.

Examples of petrified wood in Namibia. Surrounded by muck, both the wood and the muck are now stone, with distinction visible.

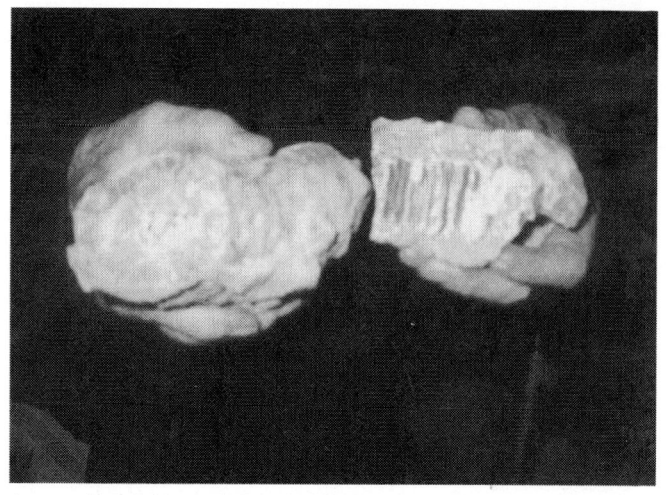

As yet unidentified by us, this fish or animal was found on the north coast of Mayo, Ireland by Fr. Des O'Sullivan. Now in a petrified state.

Much volcanic activity occurred when the earth was changing shape. Compare fountains of the great deep, which burst up as mentioned in the historical scripture. Localised eruptions as here on Mt Etna are on a much smaller scale than when the equatorial regions were expanding as the earth changed shape.

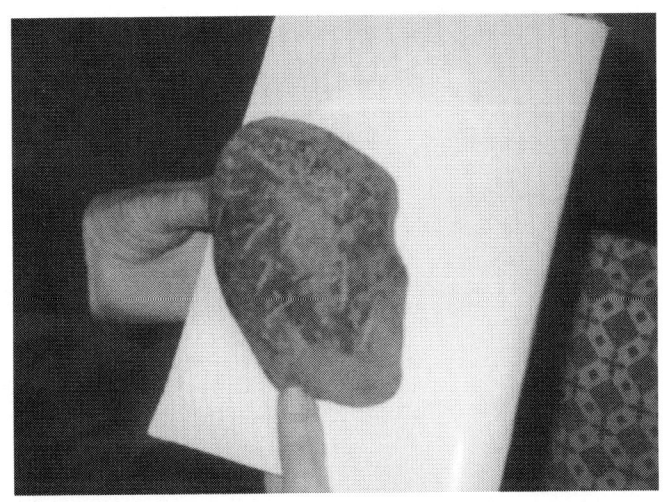

Human skull, now petrified, found in surface clay in the grounds of Kimmage Manor. Left side of head broken off – maybe by an agricultural implement: note the tracks of the harrows. Many other petrified heads et cetera have been found, but features are not as well preserved, due to movement of tides. Search for more!

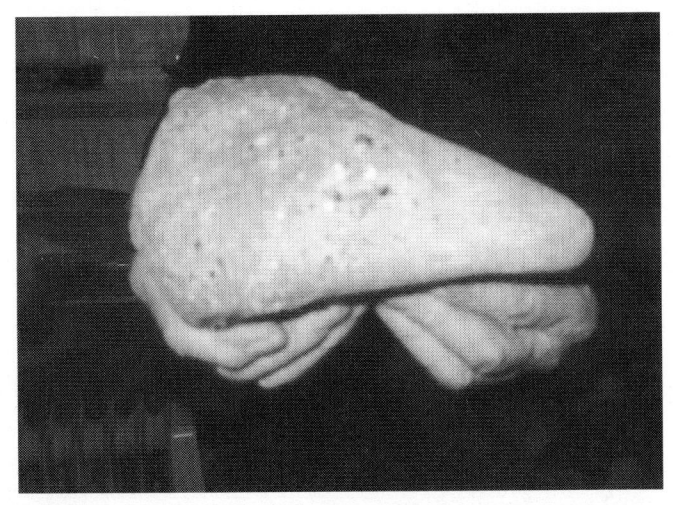

Petrified head of ostrich. Found at Greenhills, Co. Dublin, twenty-five feet down in a sand quarry. Came in float as a dead animal, sank and was petrified and was then washed out of stratum. It was then rolled around on the seabed for the length of time it takes to make sand and gravel out of broken stones. This explains why it is now somewhat rounded.

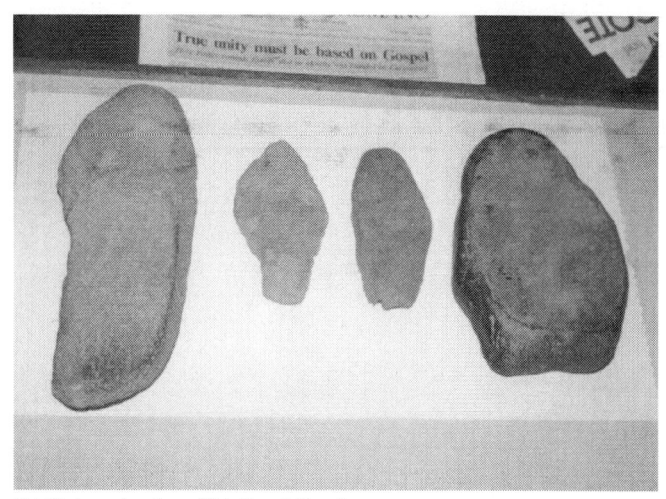

Petrified wooden shoes. Note the relative sizes.

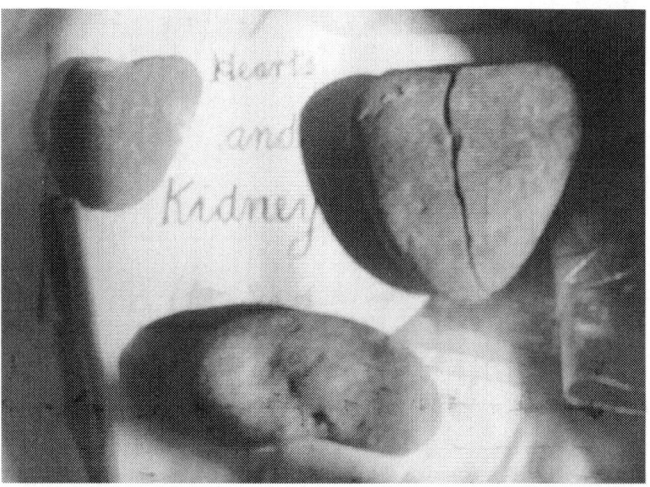

Top: two petrified hearts. Left heart somewhat crushed. Right broken. The compressed blood has been petrified and is visible from the break.
Bottom: one petrified kidney.

Appendix I

COPY OF LETTER TO IRISH NATIONAL MUSEUM ON FINDS OF HISTORICAL GEOLOGY: HUMAN, ANIMAL AND ARTEFACTS FROM AD 1961 ONWARD

Kimmage Manor
Dublin 12

To the Curators of the Irish National Museum

Gentlemen,
I expect that the petrifications that have been found lately (i.e. in the sixties) may come under your notice in the not too far distant future, and I have thought well for many reasons to commit to writing and to send to you written the general principles connected with the causes of the petrifying, the time, the appearance to be expected and the distortions to be allowed for, the history of the petrified objects, the place where found, together with the historical–geological causes that eventually placed them where they are found, and I intend to add observations.

In examining them it is well to remember that they are petrifications. Now a petrified thing, granted that it is petrified, is a stone and now nothing else but a stone and therefore it is to be treated as a stone and not to be expected to still contain traces of the not yet petrified animal organism it had before this particular individual piece of stone became a stone, though those may exist now in stone form. It is a petrification and not, except speaking freely, a fossil still perhaps containing bone-matter or teeth or hooves. In a petrification even the hoof, the bone, the flesh, the teeth, the horns, the hair or feathers are all completely and without any qualification stone, and the question is not 'what tissue is visible in it?' but 'what was this particular piece of stone made from?'

Here it is useful to lay aside the microscope or let it sit where it is for the time being, as those who are rash could lose contact with reality in identifying the origin of the stone.

The microscope distorts, it shows external surface. Now as petrifications are done in watery conditions and as water is moved by balance of weight things in it are liable to be hit up against seashells, seaweed beds, stones, trees in float, et cetera and their surfaces can be packed or studded with external things as seashells, added to this roots can feed on drowned animals, worms, maggots, et cetera which can feed on and bore holes in there, these holes can be filled with petrifiable muck or mud, like the way the ears of a petrified head are generally filled, and seashells can adhere to petrified stones afterwards, when these are released from the stratum in which they turned into stone, and things being so it can be seen how easy a thoughtless rash person could err or give an unbalanced judgement, or be unable to explain things, or keep others from investigating.

The microscope will show things much bigger than they are in reality – this is distortion by enlargement. It only shows a part at a time. If it is used to examine a man at times it will only show nails, if used to examine a petrification at times it may just show a crinoid or a barnacle. Expect this for it is normal in a sea-formed petrification. If used on a dead body it may just show a cluster of maggots, but if it does the examiner does not turn away saying this is not a body.

The central line of symmetry may help the recognising effort towards success and towards knowing what the original appearance was, for one side at least may yet retain even its exact shape. A flattened object may retain the line of its external outline and the relative size and position of its parts. A human head is generally petrified with the back or side downwards. Expect to see the lower side flattened. (Its position in the Esker or elsewhere gets separate consideration.) Two sides of flattening may converge if it got stuck in a broken layer of rock.

Weight from above, or even more weight to one side, or lying in an awkward position, or sloping ground, while it is turning into stone may add to the difficulties of identification, as things will normally get smaller under weight while decaying unless they are prevented from doing this by their hardness, as a hoof might be, or unless they are encased in stone-forming mud or other causes, but where gas is formed and enclosed it will or might push parts of bodies out and so enlarge them.

Where a human head is petrified on its back the outlines of the front view may be fairly well kept, where however it is petrified on its side the lower side may be so flat that with the push down on the upper side the finished article may, if looked at from the front, resemble the shape of a half moon, the chin completely sideways, jaws also may have less space between them, especially the lower jaws, when distorted in this manner as happens with corpses buried in clay if they are lying on their side – settlement takes place. This result of settlement has not left them as they were when alive, nor does it indicate abnormality in shape nor in faculty as, say, speech.

Should a streak of white stone be seen in a petrification this shows generally that it was petrified in strata and that the strata, still under water that is in contact with limestone, cracked, because of other causes larger than what would cause the petrified object itself to crack as a blow or burst.

Should apparent (externally) layering be seen it may be just caused by the seasonal rise and fall of a local underground pool of water after the Esker is high and dry otherwise. This apparent layering will follow water level and for things found after they were disturbed could show how they were sitting while in the gravel ridge.

Should a different type or colour of limestone appear in an otherwise continuous form-shape it will normally be due to the historic causes that were involved in making it appear to be thus. For example, one part may have been above water when it was in float, one part may have been stuck in the muck in the sea floor for a while during the time the rest of it is exposed to the sea water either before or after it petrified. One part may have been exposed to decay from its position and the other part not, and many individual circumstances may have concurred to give the finished article its present appearance. But its rounded shape and external appearance with smooth rounded edges generally come from its rolling around in water as a moving pebble as well as from what it is made from.

The sutures of the skull bones may help to determine – and, for the novice, convince him – that it is a petrification and that it is the petrified head of a human body or of an animal of some definite kind, even of some definite kind that might not have been successful in preserving its species, that might not have been very beneficial to mankind except in the early years of creation, or might have been a foe of fallen man and lost the fight or died out from hunger.

Photography, especially in black and white, may help the novice and the proficient to identify things and to detect distortion by revealing what might not to the human eye be too obvious or what might easily pass unnoticed, as for example a different shade may show where the hole for the ear had been or where distortion has put it. The long study of some things, in the beginning known to be a petrification but not identified as a particular animal or a definite part of a particular animal, can at times give no results, but when a photograph from a certain angle with light coming from a certain direction is taken the result can be similar to that of an aerial photograph taken before sunset of an ancient rath where the shadows reveal what the short-sighted five-feet-high view did not cause the person to advert to.

A large number of petrifications has been found in the Greenhills, Dublin, not because they are exclusively there but because Roadstone, a firm that amongst other things sells gravel, has been taking gravel from here and so has provided the historical geologist with a most desirable state of things for study and research when he needed it, and because the quarry or gravel pit is nearer to him than Red Bog Pit, Blessington, and he has been there oftener than in Red Bog. Greenhills is about (or was before gravel was taken away) two hundred and thirty feet above the present level of the Sea of Deluge and Red Bog is about eight hundred and fifty feet above sea level, but similar conditions prevailed at the formation of both Blessington Red Bog Pit and Greenhills Gravel Pit, and the historical geologist has found similar things in both. The people and animals are similar and they are similar to the people and animals of today. The boots they were wearing when drowned are made on the same principles but there is individual variety and style and difference and it is easy to see which was worn by a woman and which was worn by a man. There is design, there is skill, there is elegance in the making of them and those who made them either studied the human foot themselves or were following a design as tradesmen.

The turf they cut and dried the season before the universal flood shows the excellent skill of the turf cutter, shows it was not frosted between the time it was cut and the time it was dried. One shows the track of the thumb and finger of the left hand and it mocks the mental invention of a climatic ice age.

Tropical animals and fowl show the universality of the flood-sea that floated them so far. Two human boots got at Greenhills around fifty feet deep show that what we see today as Ireland's surface was not there in the twenty-fourth century BC, that our land surface was still under water, that is, after the flood came on.

As there has appeared no trace of the petrified objects being indented by neighbouring objects or objects lying on them, they were fully petrified when they were piled having been, while still under water, released from stratum in which they were petrified, rolled around for sufficient time to make sand and gravel, piled where they are found – all under water and by water.

The piles were surface-modified by the tides in the later stages of the Sea of Deluge, say between two hundred and five hundred years after the shape of the earth changed, and the Esker part of the pile came into prominence for it was less subjected to moving water – being the watershed (Uisge cior) – than other parts surrounding it. As the watersheds were being abandoned by universal water level other parts were still under tidal activity and much material was taken away and spread elsewhere, but it also was modified and made into heights and valleys by the tides, and this is how we find the surface today when we allow for the effects of weather, plants, animals and men and running water.

There was no climatic ice age. The universe is very young. The historical geology narrated by Moses in the Holy Bible is accurate and explains the changes that have given us the present earth surface, eliminating all need for a frustrating search for causes in unlimited mythical time. Vast causes have, happily for the historical geologist, done vast work in an efficient manner and in a manner satisfying to our ideas of having adequate causes to produce such and such effects and have done things in a short time – the greater the cause the shorter the time required.

The ancient, noble and thoroughly proficient historians of Ireland have given us the manner and the time various local geologic changes took place, and the pivot of their dating is when the world was drowned. They tell us the number of lakes and rivers that were here when the first major colony came, and their account harmonises with the historical geology of the world for soon after a universal flood much unweathered sand, not yet turned into surface clay, is to be expected, and sand will not retain water, nor will a surface river flow where the water can escape through sand. These excellent historians who have preserved for posterity the ancient accounts so well, though so unlike what those who live today so far away from the events have conjectured and substituted for history, narrate that many of the lakes that came into being afterwards, erupted. This is consistent with the ocean-floor sweepings when the waters prevailed beyond measure, the different layers may contain substances that shrink more than others in the process of petrifying or becoming stone allowing water to come in, then when the upper arches give way the water is squirted up, a hollow forms and by this time the soil is able to retain water. There may not as yet be any surplus water to flow off but there may for we read that some erupted and flowed.

The things and persons found are not native of Ireland, for Ireland, as we know it, was formed in and by the Sea of Deluge. The giraffes, ostriches and elephants are either tropical or subtropical and they floated here as dead bodies or carcasses and materially (not formally of course) helped to build up Ireland known afterwards as the Emerald Isle because of the richness and 'lushiousness' (lusciousness) of its green grass. We allow also of course for the igneous build-up, the cores that arrested the strata that the ocean-floor sweepings were building up or that provided shelter for the strata-forming material when, having built up on one side, it overflowed to build up on the other and continued by unifying both sides in curving layers. We allow also for the igneous rock-forming liquid that overflowed the already formed strata either boiling in a raging way under the water or pouring onward flowing broadening flows of molten rock-formed and rock-forming material (rock formed by pressure perpendicular and lateral immediately after creation, afterwards made liquid by developing heat inside the earth) over the land that had been stratified when under water but now is high and dry.

We see that the Irish race has preserved very well the appearance of early men, that when we allow for distortion and individual difference there is no change from before the universal deluge till today in men and animals nor in plants nor timber. These petrified people and things are the oldest yet got and are Sea of Deluge petrifications. We are referring here to their age as petrifications for if we look into their real age it would date from the time they came into existence and so one of these would be normally older than some others and younger than some others. If we learned from history that Old Nan was five hundred years old when she drowned we would have no difficulty in accepting the fact. If we did not know her age we would be puzzled if we tried to guess it from her petrified head, but a dating-guess is folly if it goes even a day beyond the first day of creation, it is heading for the mirage of mythical time.

Petrified things need not all be as old as the Sea of Deluge petrifications. We have a sample from the Flood of Deucalion – the front quarters of a cat and it has some of the linen bandages still on it from the time it was embalmed. It was dug up between fifty-three and sixty-eight feet below sea level. Even the fine twisted linen is petrified. We can see the possibility of finding a petrified man who would be a descendant of Noah for there were four or five major local floods since the universal flood that drowned the whole world. Deucalion's flood was about 1503 BC or eight hundred and forty-five years later than Noah's.

The form-preservation in human heads and bodies is not equally good in all, and many would beat the ability of the inexperienced to detect or accept, but some are outstanding and as a man said who was present when an animal's head was found: 'a child could see that this is a head.'

What kind of a world was it that made a universal flood possible – so great as to make the Greenhills from dry-land animals with human beings predominating in numbers over any species of animal, what kind was the antediluvian world?

If the earth stopped spinning we here in Ireland would be about six miles under water in one day's time.

Global water level is caused and maintained by balance of weight (or of gravity) and quantity of water. This balance of weight is normally more or less equidistant from surface to centre when the earth is not rotating and the base-surface of the atmosphere conforms generally to water level. When however the earth is rotating, as it is now, water level is at least twelve miles higher at the equator than it would be at the poles, and the base-surface of the atmosphere in general conforms to this new water level allowing, of course, for land mountain snow and ice.

When the Lord separated the land and the seas by causing the earth to spin the water here lowered and the water piled up at the tropics forming the great deep at the tropics; the start of the spin gave first global water movement and first global stratification some of which later became rock. This is the first pivot for dating of stratified rock and where this first stratification remains and has not been re-stratified we need not expect fossils as there were none on that day, but we allow for the possibility of animals sinking in it while it is still in the state of muck, for animals were created inside a week and it was still soft for years afterwards.

Where this was re-stratified, as much of it was many times, it was done under water and so there was the usual screening by water similar to what we can see in the beds of rivers today where coarse gravel, gathered here and there, is laid down in separate beds from fine gravel and goes with the stream, at times mixing but later being separated again.

The presence of fossils in water-formed strata generally depends rather on their shape and size than on the day they died or were drowned or were washed into the sea or sank after floating, on the distance they were moved on the sea floor before they were covered up for the last time and allowed time to petrify, and so efforts to date stratified rock from the fossils found therein are just going to mislead the short-sighted scientists or to augment the scrap heap of discarded theories, and to reduce their 'time sequence' from appearing as a book in which a man may read the age of rocks to being the time contemporaneous living things finally came to rest when dead after being moved, stratified and perhaps re-stratified many times.

And this took place quickly where things are found in a state of good preservation of form and feature as we can see from the excellent form-preservation of some of those that were washed out of stratum before the muck that surrounded them became as hard as them, or to use the conjunctive form of the pronoun, as they became or had by then become. They had gone into the stratum before decay had played havoc with their features and many of them were washed out of the stratum before the surrounding stone-forming material had become as hard as them though afterwards it became as hard as them as can be seen where it got into their ears. If these well-preserved forms had not been washed and weathered out of the stratum in a small number of years, they would perhaps be today in the solid rock, and be indistinguishable and inseparable from it, for it has hardened so much more since the waters of Noah subsided ebbing and flowing and left it above sea level to dry out as we find it and know it today, and become aware of what false results can be obtained by efforts to date places by the amount of apparent erosion that is thought to have taken place at a constant rate, and under the influence or causality of causes existing and operating today without the cooperation of salt water, currents and tides. All the world was foreshore as the Sea of Deluge receded. We dwell on what was foreshore, our river valleys were foreshore. Unless this is understood dating deductions are dangerous.

If the geologist pulls up the anchor of history he can float off anywhere in the boundless ocean of mythical time and the evolutionist can find a place for dancing to his tune on board his barge.

Reality is constant and the knowledge of reality is constant and historical narration is constant as the past is constant and real time changes only in the present, but it changes, and if a fossil is a hundred years old today it will be a hundred and one this time next year. When the geology barge sinks, down goes the evolutionist with all on board while they are safe who kept their feet on solid ground.

Reasoning about things as if the world was always as it is today in reasonably stable equilibrium can mislead, reasoning in the present about the world which is post-diluvian as if it was antediluvian or as if it had not experienced within historic time the great recorded universal flood can account for and can occasion many errors and the many reasoning pitfalls into which such a multitude of human beings have tottered, into theories that are frankly insane and viciate textbooks and demean the human intelligence which in its native state demands adequate causes to produce effects.

Were I to comment on the work done in the museum it would be to express my admiration in writing as I have done orally. I have often described the Natural History section to friends as a bird's-eye view of creation. With kindest regards to all who have given to the work their time and talents I add my encouragement to continue the good work and in spite of published work to the contrary not to imitate other museums that have built up fables artistically and exposed to view fabulous origins of men and animals.

The historic Irish nation has always held in high honour the truthful historian, and it is with disgust it looks on the works of native scholars who have insidiously substituted the deductions of strangers and the conjectures of minds diseased with theories and fashion-sodden teachings for its own native ancient unchangeable narrations. Who but fools would speculate about the peoples and doings in ancient Ireland when these things are narrated, or who starting to exist in the twentieth century of the redemption would seriously attempt to teach things at variance with the narrations of venerable antiquity because he does not see what happened as possible or thinks it out of fashion or who in his senses would turn Gaels into Celts when they themselves say they are descended from the royal house of Scitia (Scythia) or fake a different genealogy or ancestry for them or fabulate a different itinerary for them when coming to Ireland other than the one they narrate themselves? Were others watching them or were the twentieth century AD lights looking at them coming? Or can reasoning powers change past events or scraps of antiques so influence the jury as to lead them to a wrong verdict'

It is therefore of great importance to human beings in their temptations to abandon the truth of what has happened for what would appear to fit better into the mould of invented theories that the museum or its curators give no countenance in their arranging of exhibits to the fostering or perpetuations of fables or show any favour to fabulous dating or leave the solid ground of history and narrated time for the plausible conjectures and mythical interpretations of plain history of any modern scholar whosoever he be, or whatever aberrations of speculative archaeology he persists in, placing his confidence or his trust in the native scholars of younger nations whose ancestors have not preserved their continuous history nor held on to the historic origin of things.

History is needed for the correct view of things. Let us take an example: say the bones of a man are found in a grave in the flexed position, now this does not (of necessity) indicate that the person was buried in the flexed position. We know from history that some were buried standing facing their foes. These, when they sink down, normally will fall as if flexed, and when we find out they were facing in a certain direction we are given a pointer in the direction of the foe. We might know from history when hostility troubled that district and be even able to say: 'These are the bones of such a king, he died after he had reigned so many years, he was buried by his friends. He was slain by such a warrior. His grave was high enough to hold him standing up. His father was so and so of the royal line of N. and of the race of such a descendant of Noah.' History changes nameless dead bones of archaeology into persons who have lived individual lives.

It is not so easy doing all this to those drowned in a universal flood but where we find giants we can say: he was of the race of Seth on his father's side, his mother was of Cain's race. He was born between the year of one and sixteen and fifty-six but we could narrow this much more for Adam, the father of our race, the first man who was created and made from the slime of the earth directly by God, was about one hundred and thirty years old when Seth was born – old we would say today, but at that time our race was young and had not yet felt the ravages of diseases of body and mind, the evil effects of malnutrition, slavery, oppression, sins, bad education and sinister purposes. We could narrow it also on the other side where from his size and appearance we might be able to deduct fairly accurately the years of age he was when drowned, but here we have to consider that as the race was then young, strong and active in its habits, the early blighting of not yet matured beauty may have been prevented by paternal and maternal control, vigilance and loving care that safeguards youth from self-harm and gives them the protection of home life and this in face of the fact that their thoughts were bent on evil, for no parents except the mentally afflicted will tolerate blackguardism in their children, nor legislators tolerate harm to persons they care for.

It is not easy naming those drowned in the universal flood, but there are some with names not for historical identification but names such as Sean, John-Willie, Tam, Nancy, Old Nan, John-Henry, Pat, Charles and Tony to mention some that we have given them for present-day identification. It is not my intention to keep these finds secret though there is advantage in avoiding distracting sightseers while serious research and study is going on, but my attitude is to welcome help not to repel it, to understand and instruct those whose previous education made them very ill-fitted for down-to-earth facts, but convinces them with proofs, bless the mark, that they were not living intellectually on mythical theories. I have found constant vigilance necessary to keep the finds from being in any way whatsoever scraped for I am endeavouring to keep them just as I found them, otherwise if all who wanted to examine them scraped there – there is terrible tendency to scrape them in greenhorns – they would in the course of years be very nearly useless or bad sculptures, not priceless samples of early men, animals, artefacts, et cetera. It would seem that some examiners are not quite convinced that the inside of a stone is stone, or that scraping is a method of ruining the outside, and of depriving the present generation and posterity of the advantage and opportunity of seeing for themselves what these finds were like when found.

These are finds of historical geology, these things were placed in the earth by geological causes. We have been using history, following it and using what we could use in geology and any other factual knowledge acquired, human and divine, and have longed for a teacher who could tell us about these things for we saw much to be done, and, that much could be done in the science of identifying the materials from which stones in their present form were made. We also saw how easy it would be to err in these matters and how ill-equipped those who are not mentally anchored by the historical geology of the Holy Scripture and of ancient Ireland are, and how they would be working in darkness.

I have recorded the depths at which many of the finds were got but more out of condescension for the intellectual methods and fads of certain scholars than for any real scientific necessity; it may help some in the future, it does not appear to have got people far in the past as regards dating, but long ago I have seen this as a big unnecessary intellectual effort like that of a person who would examine another person's teeth, hair, eyes, skin and eyebrows to find out his age and of course err at the finish, instead of looking up his baptismal register to get the facts. It will normally give the date of his birth, the day he was given the restoration of the divine life, the full name or names he was given, the names of his parents and the names of his sponsors, and where his parents lived. This is the scientific way of doing things. A person might have changed his address many times so that finding the number of years he lived in, say, Greenhills does not give us his age. It is similar with these finds for they were restratified many times and their present position is useless for dating purposes. We have to look up the scripture for that and in it we find the time and the explanation and the details and the destruction necessary to explain so many finds.

The world was historically made in six days. It was made by God for his own glory and for man's use and benefit, and so it is foolish to read into water-screening a succession of living things as if some things were created months or years before other species were created, where it is generally a question of things existing at the same time, drowned the same six weeks, being moved here and there as water screens them until they are left where they are found. It is a foolish following of a mythical theory, a simpleton's acceptance thereof, and a taking for proof the sophistry that supports it among scholars, a wandering search for possibles where not possibles but facts are involved. What happened? We are told what happened and it is not the same as the scientistical deductions, guesses and theories, that they would try to float the possibility of on mythical time. The geology of the world is explained within historic time – not yet six thousand years ago – and these finds support that dating and confirm the fact of a universal flood. The ideal museum, as well as giving a bird's-eye view of creation, would not fail to show the great event that happened one thousand, six hundred and fifty-six years later but would strive to give a sample of each species and each strain or variety together with the artefacts, shoes, implements, turf, et cetera that those drowned wore, used or cut before they perished because of their incredulity, for they did not see the possibility of a world drowning nor where sufficient water to do it could be found. It will require field work but much has been successfully done and conditions all over Ireland are very favourable with the Sea of Deluge petrifications facing us all over the country.

If any of you want to see any of these or to have a showing of an 8 mm film on a sample of them let me be told. It runs for about one and a quarter hours and is mostly in colour – it brings in other things as well as the objects found. It is not edited, the fifty feet are just joined for I want to keep them as taken for a record. It has been shown privately many times by me with suitable commentary or instruction and explanation where and when necessary. It is good to have seen it at least once, so if you want to see it contact –

Philip Lynch
Kimmage Manor,
Dublin 12
Saint Patrick's Day, 1969

Appendix II

Gaelic is a very old language and in the long course of centuries has been used as a living language and so has admitted into its pronunciation what is referred to as aspiration. It has used this to give a smooth flow and to express gender of nouns and at times cases of nouns and following certain words, so we find:

ċ   or ch nearly equals gh (gutteral)

ḋ   or dh nearly equals y (adh = $\overline{oo}$)

ḟ   or fh is silent

ġ   or gh nearly equals y

ṁ   or mh nearly equals w if broad, v if slender

ḃ   or bh same as mh (bha = oó-a)

ṗ   or ph same as f

ṡ   or sh same as h

ṫ   or th same as h
           dl equals ll, nd equals nn

Appendix III
DATES

The solar year which is now fairly constant has not always been so. The corals in Devon, England show that after the deluge there were four hundred and five days in a solar year. This was because the rain water made the Earth heavier so that it took a wider orbit around the sun and hence forty more days travelling.

In Solon's time, in answer to a question put to him by King Croesus, he answers thus:

> Now I put the terms of man's life at seventy years. These seventy years then give twenty-five thousand, two hundred days without including the intercalary month, and if we add that month to every other year, in order that the seasons may agree the intercalary months will be thirty-five more in the seventy years and the days of these months will be one thousand and fifty. Yet in all these days of twenty-six thousand, two hundred and fifty that compose these seventy years one day produces nothing exactly the same as another (et cetera).

This gives three hundred and seventy-five days in the year then, showing that the Sea of Deluge, though well down from the time the year had four hundred and five days was still not constant as it is now (Solon lived from 640 BC to 558 BC).

The length of the day is constant, it is governed by a different law, not by weight, but because the circumference of the Earth on the side farthest away from the sun has to describe or travel a longer 'circle' than the side nearest the sun. These two journeys are harmonised by the Earth's daily rotation and its travelling speed.

Also note a change in direction by the Earth does not affect water level of the Earth as when the sun stopped in Josuah's time – the Earth just changed into circular orbit and we had no flooding as we would have had if the Earth stopped spinning but we had a longer day.

Indeed it would appear that the present AD method of calendar dating started some years after the birth of our Lord. It took the reforms of Julius Caesar and much later Pope Gregory XIII before the calendar year and sun year were harmonised. There is a hill west of Letterkenny, Co. Donegal, known as Gregory hill, and on the longest day of the year the sun can be seen sinking into the vee on top of Mount Errigal.

The ancient Irish historians count the years from the time the world was drowned, which the Hebrews record as 1656 AM to the Gaels' landing in Ireland one thousand and eighty years later. From this pivot for dating (2736 AM) they record the number of years each king reigned and we have followed that. As this counting was done in years rather than months, some degree of elasticity must be allowed for. While the native Irish all respected books of history and learning and careful recording of events this was not so with invaders. It must have been extremely difficult to record and preserve the manuscripts and to harmonise local with national records of events during sustained attacks by foreigners, who were bent on destroying learning and religion. Transport was not easy in olden times and often perilous; however, we find the sequence of kings concord in all the old manuscripts and much opposition made the length of some kings' reigns doubtful. We have found that the main events concord with facts and we have no reason to doubt their truth.

In conclusion we have every reason to believe that this elasticity of years extends to no more than a few years; hence when it was carefully recorded that certain persons lived extraordinarily long lives we have no reason to doubt the narrations of Gaelic historians.

Appendix IV

THE ORIGINS AND GENEALOGY OF THE GAELS AND OF THEIR MOST PROMINENT CINEAL (CLANS) AND RULING FAMILIES

Descendant Chart from Biblical Times to the Christian Era

```
Adam and Eve
     |
    Seth
     |
    Enos
     |
   Cainan
     |
   Malaleel
     |
    Jared
     |
   Henoch
     |
  Mathusala
     |
   Lamech
     |
Noah and Cobha
```

| Sem and Olla | Japheth and Oolibana | Cam and Olvia |

- Magog
- Bath
- Fenius Fear Saidh – King of Scitia
- Niall – Teacher of Egypt
- Gaedeal – Father of Gaels
- Esru
- Sru
- Heber Scot – Return to Scitia
- Beoghaman
- Oghaman
- Tat
- Agnomon
- Laimhfhionn – Gaels to Africa   WHITE HAND
- Heber Gluinfhinn
- Adnon Fionn
- Febric Glas
- Neanual

```
                        Naudhat
                        
                        Alldhoid
                        
                        Archada
                        
                        Defhatha
                        
                        Bratha –
                        Gaels to Spain
                        
                        Breogan

    Ith –
  Son of Breogan              Bile
```

3 KINGS OF MILESIANS DIED IN SPAIN — MIL, UICE, OCCE a IN p147

```
                        Golamh Mileadh and Scota
     Lughaidh           Their sons brought Gaels to Ireland
```

see MULLAGHANTS in map

Mal	Eireamhon	Eibhear Fionn	Ir
Eadhamhan	Irial Faidh	Conmaol	Eibhear
Logh	Eithreol	Eochaidh Faobharglas	Eibhric
Maithsin	Follan	Nuadha Deaghlaimh	Airtre
Sin	Tighearmhas	Glass	Art
Gos	Eanbhotha	Rossa	Seadhna
Eadhaman	Smior Ghall	Roitheachtach	Fiachadh Fionscothach

Eireamhon

3000 AM

SCOTI I

Logh Feidleach	Fiacha Labhrainne	Airereo Ard	Ollamh Fodla
Lachtaine	Aongas Olmucach	Cas Clothach	Cairbre
Nuadh Airgtheach	Maon	Muineamhon	Leabhraidh
Deirgthine	Rothachtach	Faildeargod	Bratha
Deaghadh Dearg	Dein	Cas Cead-chaingneach	Fionn
Eadhamhradh	Siorna Saolach	Failbhe	Siorlamh
Uilleann	Oilioll Olchaon	Roan	Airgead
Siothbholg	Giallchadh	Rochachtach	Fomhor
Daire	Nuadhat Fionn Fail	Feidlimidh	Dubh
Siothbholg	Aodhan Glas	Art Imleach	Rossa
Fear Uillne	Simeon Breac	Breasrach	Srubh
Daire	Muireadhach Bolgrach	Seadna Ionnarradh	Fionn Dearcach
Lughaidh	Fiacha Tolgrach	Duach Fionn	Glass
Mac Niadh	Duach Laghrach	Eanna Dearg	Caithfear
Mac Con	Eochaidh Buadhach	Lughaidh Iardhonn	Faobhardhil

Aongus Gaifuileach	Ughaine Mor	Eochaidh Uircheas	Faichen
Naithi	Laoghaire Lurc	Lughaidh Lamhdearg	Dubh
Eidirsceol	Oilioll Aine	Art	Sithrighe
Brandubh	Labhradh Loingseach	Oilioll	Rughruidhe
Flannan	Oilioll Bracan	Eochaidh	Cionga
Folachtach	Aongus Ollamh	Lughaidh Laighdhe	Cathbhadh
Aongus	Breasal Breoghamhan	Reachtadh Righdhearg	Fachtna
Dungus	Feargus Fortamhal	Cobhthach Caomh	Cas
Maoltuile	Feidlimidh Fortruin	Modhcorb	Aimhirgin Iarglunach
Donngal	Fearadhach Fionn	Fear Corb	Conal Cearnach
Nuadha	Criomhthan Coscrach	Adhamar Foltcaoin	Irial Glunmhar
Fionn	Mogha Art	Nia Seaghaman	Fiachadh Fionnaimhnas
Eidirsceol	Art	Ionnadmhar	Muireadhach
Fathadh	Alloid	Lughaidh Luaidne	Fionnchadh

Mac Con	Nuadhat Fallon	Cairbre Lusc	Dunchadh

Fionn	Fearadhach Foghlas	Duach Dallta Deaghaidh	Giallchadh
Fothadh	Oilioll Glas	Eochaidh Fear Aine	Cathbhadh

Donnchadh Mor	Fiachadh Forbrach	Muireadhach Muchna	Rochruidhe

Mac Raith	Breasal Breac	Loch Mor	Mal

Donnchadh Gud	Connla	Eanna Monchaoin	Cearb

Finghin	Nuadhat	Deirthine	Breasal Breac

Mac Con	Carrtan	Dearg	Tiobraide Tireach

Mac Con	Labhradh	Modh Neid	Feargus Gaileang

Finghin	Luidheach	Modh Nuadhat	Aongus Gaibhne

257 AD

Conchubhar	Oilioll	Oilioll Ollum	Fiachadh Aruidhe

Conchubhar	Seadna	Eogan Mor	Cas

Sir Fingin O' Driscoll	Iar	Fiachadh Muilleathan	Feidlimidh

Criomhthan Mor (son of Iar)	Oilioll Flan Beg (son of Fiachadh Muilleathan)	Iomchadh (son of Feidlimidh)
Aongus Osraighe	Lughaidh	Rossa
Laoghaoire Birnbuadhach	Corc	Lughaidh
Aingidh	Natfraoch	Eochaidh
Eachach Lamhdoid	Aongus – received St Patrick	Cronn Badhraoi
Gebhuan	Feidlimidh	Caolbhadh
Niadh Corb	Criomhthan	Conall
Cairbre	Aodh Dubh	Fothadh
Conall	Failbhe Flann	Maine
Ruamann Duach	The O'Sullivan Mor and the O'Sullivan Beara were descended from Finghin, a brother of Failbhe Flann and were chieftains in Kerry and West Cork.	Saran
Laighneach Faoilidh		Mongan
Bigne Caoch		Aodhan
Colman	Colga	Breasal Bealdearg
Ceannfaoladh	Natfraoch	Conchubhar
Scannlann Mor	Faolgus	Domhnall
Ronan Rioghflaith	Donngal	Blathmhac

Cronnmaol	Sneadhghus	Laighnen (children of Lear (Lir) died)
Faolan	Artghal	Eideadh
Anmchadh	Lachtna	Aongus Mor
Concearc	Buadhachan	Aongus Og
Amhalghud	Ceallachan Caisil	Echmhileadh
Feartghal	Donnchadh	Aodh
Donnghal	Saoir-bhreatach	Aongus
Cearbhal	Carrthach	Eithmhileadh
Ceallach	The McCarthy Mor– chieftains of East Munster were descended from Carrthach and they later became Earls of Desmond	Flaithbheartach
Donnchadh		Aodh Reamhar
Domhnall	Muireadhach	Dubhinnse
Giolla Phadraig	Cormac Maighe Teamhrach	Giolla Colaim
Donnchadh	Diarmuid Cille Badhaine	Rughruidhe
Domhnall	Domhnall Mor na Curre	Echmhileadh
Giolla Phadraig	Cormac Fionn	Muircheartach Rioghanach
Scannlan	Domhnall Ruadh na n'Oighbhreac	Art na Madhmann
Domhnall Clannach	Domhnall Og	Aodh

Domhnall Mor Moighe Laoisghe	Corbmac	Art
Seathfrud Bacach	Domhnall	Aodh
Seathfrud Fionn	Tadhg na Mainistreach	Domhnall Mor
Domhnall	Domhnall an Dana	Domhnall Og
Domhnall Dubh	Tadhg Liath	Aodh
Finghin	Corbmac Ladhrach	Art Ruadh
Finghin	Domhnall an Drumnin	Aodh

The descendants of Aodh are the family MacAongus or McGuinness.

| Finghin | Domhnall an Chead Iarla – Earl of Desmond |

Sean

Brian

Brian

Finghin

Tadhg

Brian

Brian Og

Brian Og

The descendants of this
line are the family of
Mac Giolla
Phadraig/Fitzpatrick

Descendant Chart of the Cinel Conal (O'Donnell Clans) of Tir Conal (Co. Donegal) and the Cinel Eoghan (O'Neill Clans) of Tir Eoghan (Co. Tyrone)

Ughaine Mor – 22nd from Eireamhon

Cobhthach Caolmbreagh

Meilge Molbhthach

Irangleo Fathach

Connla Cruaidh Cealgach

Oilioll Caisfhiaclach

Eochaidh Foltleathan

Aongus Toirmheach Teamhrach

Eana Aighneach

Labhra Luirc

Blathachta

Easamhun Eamhna

Roighnein Ruadh

Finlogha

Finn

Eochaidh Feilioch

```
                    Fineamhnas

                    Lughaidh Riabhdearg

8thyr was 1st yr of —  Criomhthan Nia Nair      MILESIAN KING OF
  Christ                                         IRELAND

                    Fearadhach Fionfachtnach ✳

                    Fiachadh Fionoluidhe    m. d - King alba

                    Tuathal Teachtmhar

                    Feidlimidh Rachtmhar

                    Conn Cead Cathach

                    Art Aonfhear

                    Cormac Mac Airt         obtained sovereignty
                                             over ALBA
                    Cairbre Liffeachair

                    Fiachadh Sreabhthuine

                    Muireadhach Tireach

                    Eochaidh Moighmheodhin

                    Niall Naoi nGiallach –
                    St Patrick brought by Niall

     Conal Gulban                    Eoghan

     Feargus Ceannfhada              Muireadhach

     Seadna                          Muircheartach Mac
                                     Earcha (mother)

     Feargus                         Domhnall Ilchealgach
```

174

Lughaidh	Aodh Uairiodhnach
Ronan	Maolfithrigh
Garbh	Maoldun
Ceannfhaolaidh	Fearghal
Maolduin	Niall Frasach
Airndealach	Aodh Doirndighe
Ceannfhaolaidh	Niall Caille
Muircheartach	Aodh Fionnlaith
Dalach a quo Clann Dalaigh	Niall Glindubh
Eighneachan	Muircheartach of the leather cloaks
Domhnall a quo O'Donnells	Domhnall of Ard Mhaca
Cathbharr	Muircheartach Midheach
Giolla Criost	Flaithbheartach an Trostain
Cathbarr	Aodh Athlamh (use of both hands)
Conn	Domhnall Ogdhamh
Tadhg	Flaithbheartach of Loch Adhar
Aodh	Conchubhar na Fiodhgha

Domhnall	Tadhg of Gleann
Donnchadh	Muircheartach of Magh Line
Eighneachan	Aodh, the lazy-limbed youth
Domhnall Mor	Niall Ruadh
Domhnall Og	Brian Cath Duin
Aodh	Domhnall
Niall Garbh	Aodh
Toirrdhealbhach an Fhiona	Niall Mor
Niall Garbh	Niall Og
Aodh Ruadh	Eoghan
Aodh Dubh	Einri
Maghnus	Conn
Rughroidhe	Conn Bacach

This line were chieftains of Cinel Conal – the O'Donnell clans in Tir Conal (modern Co. Donegal) and later became Earls of Tyrconnell. Their title was removed by Elizabeth I for rebellion.

An Fear Dorcha (his brother was Sean)

Aodh (Hugh) O'Neill – Earl of Tyrone

Sean O'Neill

This line were chieftains of Cinel Eoghan – the O'Neill clans of Tir Eoghan (Co. Tyrone) and later became Earls of Tyrone. After rebellion in 1601 Elizabeth I bestowed the title on a more amenable minor sect of the clan

Descendant Chart of the Dal Riada Chieftains and Kings of the Gaelic Kingdom of East Ulster and South-West Scotland

- Aongus Toirmheach Teamhrach – 7th from Ughaine Mor
- Fiacha Fear Mara
- Eochaidh Riada
- Earc
- Fiorted
- Fiachaidh Cathmhaol
- Eochaidh Andod
- Eagar Cearr
- Fidh Feige
- Cruithluath
- Sean Cormac
- Feidhlimidh Roineach
- Aongus Buidhneach
- Aongus Aislingtheach
- Aengus Firt
- Eochaidh Muinreamhar

```
Earc
 |
Neisi Mor
 |
Feargus
 |
Domhangort
 |
Gabhran
 |
Aodhan
 |
Eochaidh Buidhe
 |
Domhnall Breac
 |
Domhangort
 |
Aodh Fionn
 |
Eochaidh
 |
Ailpin
 |
Cinneidigh
 |
Constantin
 |
Maolcholuim
 |
Dubh
 |
Culen
 |
Constantin
```

The Dal Riada, a clan of East Ulster (Co. Antrim), conquered South-West Scotland and their combined kingdom, having lasted a long time, ended when the Scottish portion was absorbed into the Scottish nation.

Descendant Chart of the O'Connor Don and O'Connor Roe (Red)

- Eochaidh Moighmheadhin – 29th from Ughaine Mor
- Brian
- Duach Galach
- Eoghan Sreab
- Muireadhach Mal
- Feargus
- Eochaidh Tiormcharna
- Aodh
- Uadha
- Raghallach
- Feargus
- Muireadhach Muilleathan
- Muilleathan
- Ionrachtach
- Murghal
- Tomaltach
- Muirgheas

- Tadhg Mor
- Conchubhar
- Cathal
- Tadhg
- Conchubhar
- Cathal
- Tadhg an Eich Ghil
- Aodh an Gaibhearnaigh
- Ruaidhri na Soighe-Buidhe
- Toirdhealbhach Mor
- Cathal Crobhdhearg
- Aodh
- Ruaidhri
- Eoghan
- Aodh
- Feidhlimidh
- Aodh
- Toirdhealbhach-Ruadh
- Tadhg
- Cathal Ruadh
- Tadhg Buidhe

| Toirdhealbhach-Ruadh |

| Aodh |

| Cathal Og |

| Tadhg |

| Aodh |

The O'Connor Don and O'Connor Roe were chieftains in the North Midlands of Ireland. An O'Connor Don, Ruaidhri (Rory) was the last High King before the conquest by the Normans.

Descendant Chart of the O'Kelly, O'Shaughnessy, Mac Sorley, Doyle and Mac Donnell Families

Cormac Mac Airt – 25th from Ughaine Mor

Cairbre Liffeachar

Fiachadh Sraibhthine	Eochaidh Doimlen	
Muireadhach Tireach	Colla da Crioth	Colla Uais
Eochaidh Moighmheadhon	Iomchadh	Eochaidh a quo Clann Dubhghaill (Doyle)
Fiachra	Domhnall	Carrthan
Fearadhach Daithi	Eochaidh Fear Da Ghiall	Earc
Eochaidh Breac	Maine Mor	Feargus
Eoghan	Breasal	Gofraidh
Conall	Dallan	Maine
Goibhne	Lughaidh	Niallghus
Cobhthach	Fearadhach	Suibhne
Colman	Cairbre Crom	Meadhruidhe
Guaire an Einigh	Corbmac	Siolan
Artghal	Eoghan Fionn	Giolla Adhamhnain
Aodh	Diocholla	Giolla Brighde
Murchadh	Dluthach	Somhairle

Bran Leathdearg	Fithcheallach		Raghnall
Branan	Innreachtach		Domhnall a quo Clann Domhnaill
Garbhath	Oillioll		Aongus Mor
Eagna	Fionachta		Aongus
Nochbha	Ceallach a quo O'Kelly		Eoin
Sioghmuile	Aodh		Eoin Mor
Maoltuile	Murchadh		Domhnall Ballach
Cas	Tadhg an Cath Bhriain		Eoin Cathanach
Maolchiarain	Conchubhar		Alasdran
Fearghal	Conchubhar		Somhairle Buidhe
Cu Maighe	Tadhg		Raghnall
Donnchadh	Diarmuid		Raghnall
Seachnasach	Conchubhar
Goll Buidhe	Tadhg
Raghnall	Domhnall
Giolla na Naomh	Conchubhar
Eoghan	Domhnall
Sean	Tadhg
Uilliam	Tadhg

This line is the origin of the Mac Sorley, the clan Dubhghaill (Doyle) and the clan Domhnall (Mc Donnell families)

This line of descent is the origin of the O'Ceallaigh (O'Kelly) families.

- Diarmuid
- An Giolla Dubh
- Diarmuid
- Ruaidhri
- Diarmuid
- Ruidhri
- Diarmuid

The O'Shaughnessy families have their origin in this line of descent.

Eoghan – son of Niall Naoi n Giallach						
Muir-eadhach		Feargus	Oilill	Feidh-limidh	Eochaidh Binnigh
Muir-ceantac a quo Mac Lachluin	Maine	This line is the origin of the O'Connor family of Magh Ithe.	This begins the Ceallaigh (O'Kelly) family.	This line begins the O'Duibh-dhiormaid (Dagermitt and Mac Dermott) family.	Here begins the Cinel Binnigh.
His son Mongan is the origin of the Donnghaile (Donnelly) family. Muirceantac's son Feargal a quo Mac Cathmhoil (Cambell)	This line is the origin of the O'Gairm-leadhaigh (Gormley) family.				

Aodh Athlamh – 17th from Eoghan – son of Niall Naoi nGiallach	
Domhnall Ogdhamh	Fergus Fanaid
	Donnshleibhe – The Donleavy family began with this man.

The M'Conns of County Down are so-called from a Conn O'Driscoll who lived there.

Descendant Chart of the Murrough, Mac Murrough and O'Dwyer Families

Breasal Breac – 40th from Eireamhan

Luighdheach Laitfhinn

Seadna Siothbhach

Nuadhat Neacht

Feargus Fairrge

Rossa Ruadh

Fionn File

Modh Corb

Cu Corb

Nia Corb (his brother Caibre is the ancestor of the O'Dwyers)

Corbmac Gealta Gaoth

Feidlimidh Fiorurglas

Cathaoir Mor

Fiachadh Aicead

Breasal Bhealach

Labhraidh

Eanna Ceannsalach

- Criomhthan
- Naithi
- Eoghan Caoch
- Faolan
- Faolchu
- Onchu
- Ruadhghal
- Aodh
- Diarmaid
- Cairbre
- Cionaith
- Ceallach
- Domhnall
- Diarmuid
- Donnchadh Maol na mBo
- Diarmaid Mac Maol na mBo
- Murchadh
- Donnchadh
- Diarmaid na nGall

- Domhnall Caomhanach
- Domhnall
- Muircheartach
- Art
- Art Og
- Gearalt
- Domhnall Riabhach
- Art Buidhe
- Muircheartach
- Cathaor Carrach
- Donnchadh
- Domhnall Spaineach
- Sir Murchadh Mac Murrough

Descendant Chart of the Dal (People) gCais – O'Brien Clan and of the O'Meagher Clan

Oilioll Olam – 46th from Eibhear Fionn	

Corbmac Cas	Cian

Modh Corb	Tadhg

Fear Corb	Connla

Aongus Tireach	Fionnachta

Lughaidh Meann	Eochaidh Faobharghlas

Conal Eachluath	Athchu

Cas	Lughaidh

Blod (Blod's brother was Caisin and had ten other brothers)	Fiathaidh

Carrthach Fionn (his brother was Breanainn ban)	Feidlimidh

Eochaidh Bailldearg	Donn Cuan

Conall	Lughaidh

Aodh Caomh	Feargna
Cathal	Aodh Mor
Toirrdhealbheach	Meachar
Mathgamhan	Cu Choile
Annluan	Caolluidhe
Corc	Meacar
Lachtna	Dluthach
Lorcan	Tadhg
Cinneidhigh	Eigneach
Brian Boramha – Boru – (High King)	Domhnall
Tadhg	Murchadh Og
Toirrdhealbhach	Meacar
Diarmuid	Fiachaidh
Toirrdhealbhach	Iarann
Domhnall Mor	Donnchadh
Donnchadh Cairbreach	Muircheartach
Conchubhar na Suibhdhaine	Maolseachlann

Tadhg of Caoluisge	Fionn

Toirdhea-lbhach	Diarmuid

Muircheartach	Giolla na Naomh

Mathghamhan of Maonmhagh	Piaras

Brian of Cath an Aonaigh

	Giolla na Naomh

Toirdhea-lbhach	Giolla na Naomh

Tadhg	Tadhg

Toirdhea-lbhach	Giolla na Naomh

Conchubhar	Giolla na Naomh Mor

Donnchadh	Giolla na Naomh Og

Conchubhar	Tadhg

Donnchadh	Sean

| Brian | Tadhg Og |

| Henry O'Brian – Earl of Thomond |

The Dal gCais (O'Brien) were chieftains of Thomond, Co. Clare and North Munster. They held the High Kingship of all Ireland at the time of Brian Boru and later became Earls of Thomond.

Further Family Genealogies

Aongus, tenth from Oilioll Olum, a quo Muintear Loingsigh, Muintear Uainidhe, Muintear Bhreachtgha, Muintear Bhreanainn, Muintear Sheasnain, Muintear Riada, Muintear Thomraigh, Muintear Chorbmacain.

Aodh, brother of Caisin, eighth from Oilioll Olum, a quo Siol Aodha i.e. Clann Mac Con Mara and from these: Mac Flannchadha, Muintear Ghrada and Clann Caisin.

Bréanainn Ban, ninth from Oilioll Olum, a quo Muintear Urthaile, Muintear Mhaoldomnaigh, Muintear Chearnaigh.

Aongus, brother of Caisin, eighth from Oilioll Olum, a quo O'Deaghaidh, Cineal Fearmaic, Cineal Baoi and Cineal Cualochtaigh.

Aongus, a brother of Aongus and Caisin but called Aongus Ceann Nathrach, a quo Muintear Ifearnain and Muintear Neachtain.

Dealbhaoth, brother of Caisin, eighth from Oilioll Olum, a quo Muintear Mag Cochlain.

Lughaidh, brother of Caisin, eighth from Oiloll Olum, a quo Muintear Dhubhorchon and Muintear Chonraoi.

O'Connor of Glengeimhean are from Cian, third son of Oilioll Olum.

O'Connor Faly are from Rosa Failge, son of Cathaoir Mor, twelfth from Breasal Breac. The O' Dempseys and O'Duinns are also from Rosa Failge. Cathaoir Mor had thirty sons. From Fiachadh, son of Cathaoir Mor, are O'Toole, O'Byrne, O'Dowling, O'Ryan, O'Muldon, O'Cormack and O'Duffy.

From Brian, son of Eochaidh Moighmheadhin is Orbsion from whom comes O'Maille and from Earc Dearg, fifth from Cairbre Liffeachair, come O'hAinlidhe and Mac Breanain. From Feargus, fifth from Eochaidh Moighmheadhin, come O'Ruairc and also Mac Tighearnan. From Ionrachtach, twelfth from Eochaidh Moighmheadhin, is O'Birn and also O'Fallamhain. From Feidlimidh's brother Toirdhealbhach is O'Connor Donn. From Ruaidhri's brother Maolrunaidh (Ruaidhri was twenty-fourth from Eochaidh Moighmheadhin) comes MacDiarmuid of Magh Luirg from whom sprang the three Donnchadha's and MacDiarmada Ruadh.

From Cathal's brother Brian Luighneach (Cathal was twenty-sixth from Eochaidh Moighmheadhin) comes O'Conner Sligo. From Aodh Dall come the O'Gealbhuidhe. From Cathal's brother Maghnus comes Mac Maghnus of Tir Tuthail. From Conor na Midhe comes Clan Conaifne.